ADVENTURINGS IN THE PSYCHICAL

LECTOR HOUSE PUBLIC DOMAIN WORKS

ADVENTURINGS IN THE PSYCHICAL

HENRY ADDINGTON BRUCE

9 789353 422400
ISBN: 978-93-5342-240-0

First Published: 1914

LECTOR HOUSE

LECTOR HOUSE LLP
E-MAIL: lectorpublishing@gmail.com

ADVENTURINGS IN THE PSYCHICAL

BY

H. ADDINGTON BRUCE

1914

Published, April, 1914

PREFACE

THE present volume is somewhat in the nature of a sequel to "The Riddle of Personality," published six years ago. In that book I reviewed the results of modern psychological research in the realm of the abnormal and the seemingly supernormal, with the special purpose of making clear their bearings on the problem of the nature and possibilities of man. Having this special purpose in mind, it was inadvisable to attempt any topical and detailed treatment of the phenomena made the subject of scientific investigation. Such a method of treatment, no matter how it might have added to the interest of the book, would inevitably have obscured its message to the reader.

Now, however, I have undertaken this very thing, in the hope both of reinforcing the view of personality set forth in the earlier work, and of contributing something towards a wider knowledge of the progress science is making in the naturalization of the supernatural, to borrow Mr. Frank Podmore's happy phrase. Especially have I tried to bring out the exceedingly practical character of many of the discoveries made by those scientists who, despite the often contemptuous criticism of their colleagues, have valiantly persisted in their adventurings in the psychical. The world has undoubtedly been the gainer, and richly the gainer, by their labors; and it surely is well worth while to survey in some detail the field they have explored and the results of their explorations.

H. ADDINGTON BRUCE.

Cambridge, Massachusetts,
February, 1914.

CONTENTS

ADVENTURINGS IN THE PSYCHICAL

CHAPTER I

GHOSTS AND THEIR MEANING

A WITTY Frenchwoman was once asked if she believed in ghosts.

"No, not at all," was her reply. "But I am terribly afraid of them."

Most people feel precisely this way about ghosts, though few are candid enough to acknowledge it. In broad daylight, or when seated before a cheery fire among a group of congenial friends, it is easy to be skeptical, and to regard ghosts as mere products of imagination, superstition, credulity, hysteria, or indigestion. But it is notorious that even the most skeptical are liable to creepy sensations and sometimes outright panic if they experience "uncanny" sights or sounds in the darkness of the night, or in lonely, uninhabited places. Churchyards have never been popular resorts of those who go for a stroll in the cool of the evening. And let a house once get the reputation of being "haunted," it is next to impossible to find tenants for it.

Yet this almost universal attitude is entirely and fundamentally wrong. There is no reason for being afraid of ghosts, and there are many reasons for believing in them.

I do not, of course, mean to say that all ghosts are real ghosts. There are plenty of bogus ghosts, and there always will be, as long as men eat and drink too much, play practical jokes on one another, and allow their houses to become run down and infested by rats and mice.

A single rat, scampering at midnight over the loose planks of an old attic, has often been quite sufficient to produce a counterfeit "poltergeist," or troublesome ghost, of a highly impressive character. So, too, a pillow-slip swaying from a clothesline is apt to seem most ghostly to a gentleman returning home from a late supper. Ghosts, like much else in this amazing world of ours, have to be pretty sharply scrutinized.

And the point is that, after centuries of contemptuous neglect, they have at last been made the subject of investigation by men and women competent for the task—persons trained in the cautious methods of scientific inquiry, and insisting upon the strictest evidential standards, but devoid of prejudice or prepossession.

Their researches are still in progress, but they have already demonstrated that amid a multitude of sham ghosts there are perfectly authentic apparitions, displaying credentials too convincing to be denied.

What is still more important, the labors of these scientific ghostologists—especially of those enrolled in the famous English Society for Psychical Research—have also resulted in throwing much light on the nature, origin, and habits of real ghosts.

Usually, it seems, a genuine ghost is seen or heard but once or twice, and then, having accomplished its purpose, it departs to return no more. But there are plenty of well-attested cases in which a ghost attaches itself to a house or family, and keeps up its haunting for years, sometimes for centuries.

Take, for example, an experience that befell Miss Goodrich-Freer, at the time a most active member of the Society for Psychical Research, in Hampton Court Palace. This old building is unquestionably one of the most famous of all haunted houses. It dates back to the time of the first Tudors, and according to tradition is haunted by several ghosts, notably the ghosts of Jane Seymour, Henry VIII's third queen; Catharine Howard, whose spirit is said to go shrieking along the gallery where she vainly begged brutal King Henry to spare her life; and Sybil Penn, King Edward VI's foster-mother. Twice of late years the Howard ghost—or something that passed for it—has been heard, once by Lady Eastlake, and once by Mrs. Cavendish Boyle. The latter was sleeping in an apartment next to the haunted gallery—which has long been unoccupied and used only as a storeroom for old pictures—when she was suddenly awakened by a loud and most unearthly shriek proceeding from that quarter, followed immediately by perfect silence. Lady Eastlake's experience was exactly similar.

Both ladies, of course, may have heard a real shriek, possibly coming from some nightmare-tormented occupant of the palace. But no explanation of this sort is adequate in the case of Miss Goodrich-Freer, who passed a night at Hampton Court for the sole purpose of ascertaining whether or not there was any foundation for its ghostly legends.

The room she selected for her vigil was one especially reputed to be haunted, and opened into a second room, the door between the two, however, being blocked by a heavy piece of furniture. Thus the only means of entrance into her room was by a door from the corridor, and this she locked and bolted. After which, feeling confident that nothing but a real ghost could get in to trouble her, she settled down to read an essay on "Shall We Degrade Our Standard of Value?" a subject manifestly free from matters likely to occasion nervousness.

In fact, the essay was so dull that by half past one Miss Goodrich-Freer, not able to keep awake longer, undressed, dropped into bed, and was almost instantly asleep. Several hours later she was aroused by a noise as of some one opening the furniture-barricaded door. At this she put out her hand to reach a match-box which she knew was lying on a table at the head of the bed.

"I did not reach the matches," she reports. "It seemed to me that a detaining hand was laid on mine. I withdrew it quickly and gazed around into the darkness.

Some minutes passed in blackness and silence. I had the sensation of a presence in the room, and finally, mindful of the tradition that a ghost should be spoken to, I said gently: 'Is any one there? Can I do anything for you?' I remembered that the last person who entertained the ghost had said: 'Go away, I don't want you,' and I hoped that my visitor would admire my better manners and be responsive. However, there was no answer, no sound of any kind."

Now Miss Goodrich-Freer left the bed and felt all around the room in the dark, until satisfied that she was alone. The corridor door was still locked and bolted; the piece of furniture against the inner door was in place. So she returned to bed. Almost at once a soft light began to glow with increasing brightness. It seemed to radiate from a central point, which gradually took form and became a tall, slender woman, moving slowly across the room. At the foot of the bed she stopped, so that the amazed observer had time to examine her profile and general appearance.

"Her face," Miss Goodrich-Freer says, "was insipidly pretty, that of a woman from thirty to thirty-five years of age, her figure slight, her dress of a soft, dark material, having a full skirt and broad sash or soft waistband tied high up almost under her arms, a crossed or draped handkerchief over the shoulders and sleeves which I noticed fitted very tight below the elbow. In spite of all this definiteness I was conscious that the figure was unsubstantial, and felt quite guilty of absurdity in asking once more: 'Will you let me help you? Can I be of any use to you?'

"My voice sounded preternaturally loud, but I felt no surprise at noticing that it produced no effect upon my visitor. She stood still for perhaps two minutes, though it is very difficult to estimate time on such occasions. Then she raised her hands, which were long and white, and held them before her as she sank upon her knees and slowly buried her face in the palms in an attitude of prayer—when quite suddenly the light went out, and I was alone in the darkness.

"I felt that the scene was ended, the curtain drawn, and had no hesitation in lighting the candle at my side.... The clock struck four."

Again investigation showed that the corridor door was locked and bolted as she had left it, and the inner door still firmly barricaded. Consequently, skeptical though she had been when she arrived at Hampton Court Palace, Miss Goodrich-Freer in leaving it entertained no doubt that she had witnessed a genuine psychical manifestation.

The same conclusion was forced upon two ladies, Miss Elizabeth Morison and Miss Frances Lamont, in connection with a visit paid by them to another famous haunted house, the Petit Trianon at Versailles, the favorite summer home of that unfortunate queen Marie Antoinette, whose ghost, as well as the ghosts of her attendants, has long been alleged to be visible at times in and around it. Miss Morison and Miss Lamont had been sightseeing in the royal palace, but tiring of this had set off, in the early afternoon, to walk to the Trianon. Neither of them knew just where it was located, but taking the general direction indicated on Baedeker's map, they finally came to a broad drive, which, had they only known it, would have led them directly to their destination. As it was, they crossed the drive and went up a narrow lane through a thick wood to a point where three paths diverged. Here they began to have a series of experiences which, comparatively insignificant in themselves, had a sequel so amazing that it would be incredible were it not that the veracity of both ladies has been established beyond question.[1]

Ahead of them, on the middle path, they saw two men clad in curious, old-fashioned costumes of long, greenish coats, knee breeches, and small, three-cornered hats. Taking them for gardeners, they asked to be shown the way, and were told to go straight ahead. This brought them to a little clearing that had in it a light garden kiosk, circular and like a bandstand, near which a man was seated. As they approached, he turned his head and stared at them, and his expression was so repellent that they felt greatly frightened. The next instant, coming from they knew not where, and breathless as if from running, a second man appeared, and speaking in French of a peculiar accent, ordered them brusquely to turn to the right, saying that the Trianon lay in that direction. Just as they reached it, they were again intercepted, this time by a young man who stepped out of a rear door, banged it behind him, and with a somewhat insolent air guided them to the main entrance of the palace.

While they were hurrying thither, Miss Morison noticed a lady, seated below a terrace, holding out a paper as though reading at arm's length. She glanced up as they passed, and Miss Morison, observing with surprise the peculiar cut of her gown, saw that she had a pretty "though not young" face.

"I looked straight at her," she adds in the published statement she has made regarding their adventure, "but some indescribable feeling made me turn away, disturbed at her being there."

Afterwards this "indescribable feeling" was accounted for when Miss Morison identified in a rare portrait of Marie Antoinette the lady she had seen seated below the terrace!

Still more remarkable, subsequent visits to the Trianon brought to both ladies the startling knowledge that the actual surroundings of the place and the place itself differ vastly from what they saw that summer afternoon. The woods they entered are not there, and have not been there in the memory of man; the paths they trod have long been effaced; there is no kiosk, nor does anybody living, except Miss Morison and Miss Lamont, remember having seen one in the Trianon grounds; on the very spot where Miss Morison saw the lady in the peculiar dress a large bush is growing; and the rear door, out of which stepped the young man who guided them around to the front, opens from an old chapel that has been in a ruinous condition for many years, the door itself being "bolted, barred, and cobwebbed," and unused since the time of Marie Antoinette.

On the other hand, their personal researches in the archives of France have brought to light so many confirmatory facts that both Miss Morison and Miss Lamont are firmly persuaded that the Trianon, its environment, and its people

[1] In a prefatory note to the book, "An Adventure," in which these ladies detail their experience, their publishers, Messrs. Macmillan and Company, of London, guarantee "that the authors have put down what happened to them as faithfully and accurately as was in their power." Their good faith is also vouched for by a reviewer in The Spectator.

were once exactly as they appeared to them; and that in very truth they saw the place as it looked, not at the time they first visited it, but in the closing years of the French Monarchy, more than a century before.

That historic German ghost, the White Lady of the Hohenzollerns, would likewise seem to have more than a legendary basis. Her mission, apparently, is to announce the death of some member of the Hohenzollern family, and her most frequent haunting-place is the royal palace at Berlin. She was seen as early as 1628, and since the time of Frederick the Great her appearance has been regularly chronicled on the eve of the death of the King of Prussia.

For the matter of that, there are not a few families whose ancestral homes, according to tradition, are haunted by death-announcing ghosts. This is particularly the case with certain distinguished British families. Two white owls perching on the roof of the family mansion are taken as a sure omen of death in the Arundel of Wardour family. The Yorkshire Middletons, a Catholic family, are said to be warned of approaching death by the apparition of a Benedictine nun. Equally noteworthy as a spectral messenger of tragedy is the so-called Drummer of Cortachy Castle, a Scottish ghost that haunts the ancient stronghold of the Ogilvys, Earls of Airlie, but is in evidence only when an Ogilvy is about to die.

The story goes that, hundreds of years ago, when the Scots were little better than barbarians, a Highland chieftain sent a drummer to Cortachy Castle with a message that was not at all to the liking of the Ogilvy of that time. As an appropriate token of his displeasure, he seized the luckless drummer, stuffed him into his drum—he must have been a very small drummer, and have carried a very big drum—and hurled him from the topmost battlements of the castle, breaking his neck.

Just before he was tossed off, the drummer threatened to make a ghost of himself, and haunt the Ogilvys forevermore. He has been, it would seem, as good as his word. Every once in a while ghostly drumming is heard at Cortachy Castle, and always the death of an Ogilvy follows. An especially impressive account of one instance of this peculiar and most unpleasant haunting has been left by a Miss Dalrymple, who happened to be a guest at Cortachy during Christmas week of 1844.

It was her first visit to the Castle, and she was entirely unaware of the existence of the family ghost. On the evening of her arrival, while dressing for dinner, she was startled by hearing under her window music like the muffled beating of a drum. She looked out, but could see nothing, and presently the drumming died away. For the time she thought no more of it, but at dinner she turned to her host, the Earl of Airlie, and asked:

"My lord, who is your drummer?"

His lordship made no reply, Lady Airlie became exceedingly pale, and several of the company, all of whom had heard the question, looked embarrassed. Realizing that she had made a slip of some sort, Miss Dalrymple quickly changed the subject, but after dinner, naturally feeling somewhat curious, she brought it up with one of the younger members of the family, and was answered:

"What! Have you never heard of the Drummer of Cortachy?"

"No," said she. "Who in the world is he?"

"Why, he is a person who goes about playing his drum whenever there is a death impending in our family. The last time he was heard was shortly before the death of the late countess, the earl's first wife, and that is why Lady Airlie turned so pale when you mentioned it."

The next night Miss Dalrymple heard the drumming again, and, falling into a panic when she learned that nobody else had heard it, hurriedly left Cortachy Castle. But the drumming was not for her. True to tradition, the drummer was concerned only with announcing the death of an Ogilvy, one of whom, the Lady Airlie who had been so disturbed by Miss Dalrymple's question, died soon afterward while on a visit to Brighton.

Five years later the drumming was once more heard, this time by an Englishman who had been invited to spend a few days with the Earl of Airlie's oldest son, Lord Ogilvy, at a shooting box near Cortachy. Crossing a gloomy moor, in company with an old Highlander, the Englishman suddenly stopped, and, with a look of amazement, exclaimed:

"What can a band be doing in this lonely place? Has Lord Ogilvy brought a band with him?"

The Highlander glanced at him strangely.

"I hear naething," he said.

"Why, yes, can't you hear it? A band playing in the distance—or at any rate, somebody playing a drum."

"An' is it a drum ye hear?" cried the Highlander. "Then 'tis something no canny."

In another moment the lighted windows of the shooting box came into view, and the Englishman hastened forward, fully expecting to have the mystery solved. But he found no musicians—only a scene of considerable confusion. Lord Ogilvy, it appeared, had just started for London, summoned by news that his father was dangerously ill.

And the very next day, as the Englishman's Highlander guide was not at all surprised to learn, the Earl of Airlie died.

Of all family ghosts, however, none is so strongly substantiated by documentary[2] evidence as the Knocking Ghost of the Basil Woodds, an old English family. This ghost began operations about the time of the Stuart Restoration, and it is alleged has ever since continued to announce, by three or more loud knocks, the approaching death of a Basil Woodd. First-hand and thoroughly trustworthy accounts are extant of its activity in quite recent times.

December 15, 1893, Mr. Charles H. L. Woodd died at Hampstead, England,

[2] The documents in this case are published in the Proceedings of the Society for Psychical Research, vol. xi, pp. 538-542.

after a brief illness. The night before he died the Knocking Ghost was heard by two persons, at Hampstead by his daughter, and in London by his son, the Reverend Trevor Basil Woodd. Both have made statements describing their singular experiences.

"On Thursday evening, December 14, 1893, after church," says the Reverend Mr. Woodd, "I was sitting before my fire. I knew my father was ill, and had a presentiment that he was dangerously ill, though if I had known this I should have remained at Hampstead, where I had been that day. As I sat, I distinctly heard three knocks, perhaps more, like the sound of some one emptying a tobacco pipe upon the bars of my fire grate.

"Thinking it might be a warning, I did not go to bed for an hour, fearing I would be sent for. At one A. M. I was awakened by a ringing of the front door-bell and knocking. It was my father's butler, who told me the doctor had sent for me, as my father was very ill. I said to my housekeeper:

"'I must go. I feel sure that my father is dying, because I heard the Woodd knocks, as I sat in my chair before going to bed.'

"On my arrival my first question was: 'Is he still alive?' for I believed he must have passed away at the time of the knocking. He died at eight-forty-five next morning."

Mr. Woodd's housekeeper corroborates this statement. As to the knocking heard at Hampstead, the daughter, Mrs. Winifred Dumbell, testifies:

"On December 14, 1893, Thursday morning, hearing my father, Mr. Charles Woodd, was not well, I left Epsom, where I had been staying, for Hampstead, and found my father in bed and very weak, but I was in no way anxious about him, as I did not suppose him to be seriously ill. At eleven o'clock at night, being tired and finding I could not assist my mother or the nurse, I lay down in an adjoining room, leaving the door wide open, and fell asleep.

"In a short time I was suddenly awakened by a loud rapping as if at the door. I jumped up and ran into the passage, thinking my mother had called me. I listened at the door of my father's room, but no one was moving. I lay down again and instantly fell asleep, when exactly the same thing occurred. I did not actually sleep again, and cannot say whether any sound made me get up the third time, but I went in search of the doctor and gathered that he was anxious about my father, who was getting much weaker. We were all aroused, and about eight o'clock A. M. my father died.

"I did not connect this rapping with the Woodd warning, as all was so sudden and unexpected, but on mentioning it at breakfast the next morning to my brother, the Reverend Trevor Basil Woodd, he told me he also heard a similar warning in his rooms at Vauxhall Bridge Road about the same time."

To mention only one other of the many instances that might be cited, the Knocking Ghost was again heard on June 3, 1895, just twenty-four hours before the death of Mr. Thomas Basil Woodd at Hampstead. Again, too, it was heard by more than one person and in more than one place, by Mr. Woodd's daughters,

Fanny and Kate, and by his niece, Miss Ethel G. Woodd, who was at the time visiting friends in Yorkshire, and at first mistook the Knocking Ghost for somebody hammering nails into the wall of the next room. Oddly enough, this was also the way it sounded to Fanny Woodd, in London, as appears from the following statement signed by her:

"On June 3, 1895, at ten-thirty P. M., Fanny Woodd, staying with Mrs. Stoney, 83 Wharton Road, West Kensington, heard knocks, apparently from next door, as of nails being hammered in and pictures hung, which seemed so unlikely at that hour of night that the next morning she mentioned it to Mrs. Stoney, whose bedroom was just below hers, asking if she had heard it or could account for it."

But Mrs. Stoney had heard nothing, and the next-door neighbor, Mrs. Harriet Taylor, rather tartly declared that: "There has been no putting up of pictures or knocking of any sort in this house for quite two years. We are also early risers, and are always in bed and asleep by ten P. M." That same day Miss Woodd rejoined her father and sister in Hampstead, and was astonished to hear that the latter had been awakened about half past ten the previous night by loud knockings against the window shutters.

A few hours more and the mystery was solved by the startlingly sudden death of Mr. Woodd, from an attack of apoplexy. The Knocking Ghost of the Basil Woodds had lived up to its reputation.

The giving of death warnings is by no means confined to family ghosts, as may be sufficiently indicated by relating an incident that happened in Canada some years ago, and that has always impressed me as one of the best ghost stories I have ever heard. It was told me by an actor in the strange little drama, and knowing as I do the persons concerned, I have not the slightest hesitation in vouching for its authenticity, incredible though the reader may be inclined to regard it.

In this instance the ghost was seen by a clergyman, the Reverend John Langtry, who afterward became a prominent dignitary of the English Church in Canada. His home was in Toronto, but on the occasion of the ghostly visitation he was at the house of a Mr. and Mrs. Ruttan, who lived with their only child, a young girl, in a small town some fifty or sixty miles north of Toronto. Mr. Ruttan was another Church of England clergyman, and was a warm friend of Doctor Langtry's. This time, however, the latter had journeyed to see him simply on a matter of diocesan business, and was anxious to complete it and get back to Toronto.

To his disappointment he found that Mr. Ruttan had been called out of town, and would not be home until a late hour, possibly not until the following day. On the chance that he might return earlier than expected, Doctor Langtry accepted Mrs. Ruttan's invitation to spend the evening with her.

As they were chatting together—she being so seated that her back was toward the door leading from the parlor, whereas Doctor Langtry's position gave him a full view of the hall—she noticed that all at once he stopped in the middle of a sentence, leaned forward, and stared fixedly into the hall. She instantly turned her head, and followed the direction of his gaze, but could see nothing.

"What is the matter, Doctor Langtry?" she asked. "What are you looking at?"

"Nothing, nothing," he muttered, recovering himself with an effort. "I fancied for a moment—"

He paused, then changed the conversation. But Mrs. Ruttan—from whom I got the story—saw that from time to time he glanced furtively into the hall, and finally half rose from his seat, his face white, his limbs trembling.

"Doctor Langtry!" was her startled exclamation. "Are you ill? Whatever is the matter?"

"Oh," he said shortly, "it is only a momentary faintness. I shall be all right presently. The fatigue of the journey must have unstrung me. I will trouble you to get me a glass of water, and then I think I will return to the hotel."

He drank the water, and rose to go. But when near the front door, he turned to Mrs. Ruttan, and said:

"I don't believe I have asked after your daughter. I trust she is well?"

"She is quite well, thank you. I put her to bed just before you came in."

With his hand on the knob of the door, Doctor Langtry again paused irresolutely.

"If it's not too much trouble," he asked, "I wish you would go up-stairs and make sure she is all right now."

Wondering at his request and at his manner, Mrs. Ruttan complied, and presently returned to report that the child was sleeping peacefully. Doctor Langtry bowed with an air of obvious relief, bade her good night, and left the house. But next day, after he had transacted his business, and was about to start for Toronto, he said to Mr. Ruttan, who had accompanied him to the train:

"Ruttan, if your little girl should happen to fall ill while away from home, go to her at once, and take Mrs. Ruttan with you, even if you have no reason to feel that the illness is serious."

Mr. Ruttan laughed.

"Of course we would go to her. You may be sure of that. But why—"

"Ask me no questions," said Doctor Langtry, "but bear my request in mind if the occasion should arise."

Within a very short time the child, visiting an aunt in a near-by town, was taken ill, failed rapidly, and died almost before her parents, who had been hastily telegraphed for, could reach her bedside. Doctor Langtry's warning immediately recurred to them, and they wrote him, beseeching an explanation.

"The reason I was anxious about your little girl," he then told them, "was because the night I was sitting with Mrs. Ruttan I saw an angel enter the hall, pass up the stairs, and return, carrying the child in its arms."

But the kind of ghost most frequently seen is that which appears not before but immediately after, or coincidental with, a death. Its purpose is not to give warning of impending tragedy, but to convey the news of a tragedy already consummated. There are thousands of instances of this sort, so well authenticated as to compel credence. Not long ago an interesting case was reported to me by a gentleman living in Burlington, Vermont, the nephew of the lady—a Mrs. Hazard of Newport, Rhode Island—who saw the ghost.

She was ill at the time, and under the care of a trained nurse. One afternoon, her physician having allowed her to sit up for a couple of hours, she was seated in a chair by the side of her bed, when the nurse noticed her open wide her eyes and turn her head as if following the movements of some one. Then she heard her say, in a tone of surprise:

"Hello! Hello! There he goes! There he goes!"

As far as the nurse could see, nobody was in the room with them. But, not wishing to alarm her patient, she merely asked:

"Who is it, Mrs. Hazard?"

"Chet Keech. But he doesn't see me. And now he's gone."

Later in the day the nurse mentioned the incident to Mrs. Hazard's daughter, asking her if she knew anybody by the name of Chet Keech.

"Why, certainly I do," was the reply. "He is my cousin, and lives in Danielson, Connecticut."

That day Chet Keech had died at Danielson, as a letter informed the Hazards next morning.

Consider also this statement[3] by the Reverend C. C. McKechnie, a Scotch clergyman:

"I was about ten years of age at the time, and had for several years been living with my grandfather, who was an elder in the Kirk of Scotland and in good circumstances. He was very much attached to me and often expressed his intention of having me educated for a minister in the Kirk. Suddenly, however, he was seized with an illness which in a couple of days proved mortal.

"At the time of his death, and without my having any apprehension of his end, I happened to be at my father's house, about a mile off. I was leaning in a listless sort of way against the kitchen table, looking upward at the ceiling and thinking of nothing in particular, when my grandfather's face appeared to grow out of the ceiling, at first dim and indistinct, but becoming more and more complete until it seemed in every respect as full and perfect as I had ever seen it.

"It looked down upon me, as I thought, with a wonderful expression of tenderness and affection. Then it disappeared, not suddenly but gradually, its features fading and becoming dim and indistinct, until I saw nothing but the bare ceiling. I spoke at the time of what I saw to my mother, but she made no account of it, thinking, probably, it was nothing more than a boyish vagary. But in about fifteen or twenty minutes after seeing the vision, a boy came running breathless to

[3] First published in the Proceedings of the Society for Psychical Research, vol. x, p. 240.

my father's with the news that my grandfather had just died."

Even more remarkable was the experience of an Illinois physician, Doctor J. S. W. Entwistle, a resident of one of the Chicago suburbs. Hurrying one morning to catch a train Doctor Entwistle saw approaching him an acquaintance, once well-to-do, who had ruined himself by drink. Glancing at him as they met, the physician noticed that his clothing was torn and his face bruised, and that there was a cut under one eye. He noticed, too, that the other kept looking steadily at him with a "woe-begone, God-forsaken expression." Had he not been in such a hurry, he would have stopped and spoken to him, but as it was he passed him with a nod.

At the station Doctor Entwistle met his brother-in-law, and said, while the train was drawing in:

"Oh, by the way, I just saw Charlie M., and he was a sight. He must have been on a terrible tear."

"I wonder what he's doing in town, anyway?" commented the brother-in-law.

"I suppose he was going to see his wife."

"Not a bit of it. She won't have him around."

Then the subject was dropped, and nothing more was said about it until after they had reached Chicago. Both men, as it happened, had business at the Grand Pacific Hotel and went directly there from the train. They were met by a mutual friend, who had a copy of the Chicago *Tribune* in his hand.

"Hello," he greeted them. "Did you know that Charlie M. is dead? Here is a notice in the paper, stating that his body is at the morgue. He was killed in a saloon fight. The paper hasn't got the name quite right, but from the description it's Charlie, sure enough."

"But he can't be dead," said Doctor Entwistle, aghast, "for it was only a few minutes ago that I met him on the street in Englewood."

Nevertheless, it turned out that Charlie M. *was* dead, and that his body had been taken to the morgue several hours before Doctor Entwistle thought he saw him in the Chicago suburb. Moreover, on inquiry it was learned that the clothes worn by him when he was killed and the marks on his face "tallied in every particular with the description given by the doctor."

Quite a similar experience occurred to Mr. Harry E. Reeves when he was choirmaster at St. Luke's Church in San Francisco. On a Friday, about three in the afternoon, Mr. Reeves was in an up-stairs room at his home. He had been working on some music. Wishing to rest for a few minutes, he threw himself on a lounge, but almost immediately an unaccountable impulse led him to get up again and open the door of his room.

Standing at the head of the stairs he saw Edwin Russell, a member of his choir and a well-known San Francisco real estate broker. Mr. Russell had promised to call on him the following day to look over the music for Sunday, and Mr. Reeves's first thought was that he had come a day earlier than intended. He advanced to greet him, when, to his amazement and horror, the figure on the stairs turned as though to descend, and then faded into nothingness.

"My God!" gasped Reeves, and fell forward.

A door below was hastily opened, and two women and a man ran to his aid. The women were his sister and niece, the man was a Mr. Sprague. They found Mr. Reeves seated on the stairs, his face white and covered with perspiration, his body trembling.

"Uncle Harry!" cried the niece. "What in the world is the matter?"

Mr. Reeves was in such a panic that he could hardly speak, but he managed to reply:

"I have seen a ghost!"

"Whose ghost?" inquired Mr. Sprague, with a skeptical smile.

"The ghost of Edwin Russell."

Instantly the smile left Mr. Sprague's face.

"That's strange," said he, "that's very strange. For, as these ladies will tell you, I came to consult with you regarding the music for Mr. Russell's funeral. He had a stroke of apoplexy this morning, and died a few hours ago."[4]

Sometimes ghosts of this type present themselves in such a way as to leave no doubt as to the fact and manner of the death of the person seen. As striking a case in point as has come to my knowledge is afforded by the singular experience of an old friend of mine, Edward Jackson, son of the late General Jackson, of Bideford, England.

Born in India, Jackson was from his boyhood of a roving and adventurous disposition. He went in for all forms of athletics, more particularly boxing, cricket, and polo, and before he left India was one of the best known and most popular men in the younger sporting set.

He was still in his early twenties when he came to the United States, drifting West to go on a ranch in Wyoming. Tiring of this, though not of his fondness for adventure, he found work in a Lake Superior mine, where his quickly demonstrated ability to take care of himself in a rough-and-tumble encounter won him the position of superintendent over a gang of men whom it had hitherto been most difficult to superintend.

As superintendent he was privileged to live by himself in a small, two-room cabin, somewhat neater and more comfortable than the ordinary sleeping-shacks. It was in this cabin that he saw the ghost.

"I had returned from the mine one evening, thoroughly tired out," he said, in telling me the story, "and sat down to rest for a few minutes before an open fire. While I was sitting there, half dozing, I felt a cold current of air, and looked up, thinking that somebody had thrown the door open.

"The door was not open, but standing between me and it was the figure of

[4] Detailed reports of this case are published in the Proceedings of the Society for Psychical Research, vol. viii, pp. 214-218.

a young man whom I instantly recognized as a boyhood chum in India. He was dressed in polo costume—we had often played the game together—but for a moment I forgot all about the incongruity between his dress and the rough, outlandish place in which I then saw him. I jumped up, exclaiming:

"'By Jove, Jack, I'm glad to see you. When did you get here? And how—'

"I stopped. He had been standing with his profile toward me. Now he turned, facing me, and I saw that he was ghastly white, with a deep cut over one eye. Without a word he walked past me, gazing at me solemnly, and disappeared in the inner room.

"I don't think I am a coward, but I confess that for a moment I felt faint. Recovering, and believing that somebody must be playing me a trick, I made a dash after him.

"There was no one there—and no way in which anybody could have got out unknown to me.

"That night I wrote to my father, telling him what had happened. In his reply he informed me that my friend had been killed the same day that I saw him in my cabin on the shore of Lake Superior. He had been playing polo in far-away India, had been thrown from his horse, and had struck on his head, sustaining a wound similar to that I had seen in my vision."

Of a somewhat different order, and at once recalling to mind the adventure of Miss Morison and Miss Lamont at the Petit Trianon, is an instance reported by an Englishwoman whose name must be withheld, for reasons that will become obvious. With her husband she had recently moved into a fine old mansion surrounded by a splendid park, with a broad stretch of lawn between the trees and the house. The place had for many years been the home of a family of ancient lineage.

One night, shortly after eleven o'clock, when Mrs. M., as I shall call her, had gone to her bedroom, she thought she heard a moaning sound, and some one sobbing as though in great distress. Mr. M. was away from home, the servants slept in another part of the house, and she was quite alone except for a friend who had come to keep her company during her husband's absence, and to whom she had said good night a few minutes before. But being a courageous woman, she resolved to make an investigation and soon located the sound as coming from outdoors. Tiptoeing over to a window on the staircase landing, she raised the blind and cautiously peered out.

Below, on the lawn, in the pale glow of the moon, she saw an amazing scene. A middle-aged man, stern of face and wearing a general's uniform, was standing menacingly over a young girl, who, with hands clasped in anguish, was on her knees before him. At the sight of his hard, unrelenting expression, Mrs. M.'s one thought was not of fear for herself but pity for the unfortunate girl.

"So much did I feel for her," she said, in narrating the affair, "that without a moment's hesitation I ran down the staircase to the door opening upon the lawn to beg her to come in and tell me her sorrow."

When she reached the door, the figures of the soldier and the girl were still plainly visible on the lawn, and in precisely the same attitude. But at the sound of her voice they disappeared.

"They did not vanish instantly," Mrs. M. explained, "but more like a dissolving view—that is, gradually. And I did not leave the door until they had gone."

Months afterwards, when calling with her husband at a neighboring house, she noticed on the wall the portrait of a distinguished-looking man in a military uniform. At once she recognized it.

"That," she told her husband, in an undertone, "is a picture of the officer I saw on the lawn."

Aloud she asked: "Whose portrait is that?"

"Why," replied her host, "it is a portrait of my uncle, General Sir X. Y. He was born and died in the house you now occupy. But why do you ask?"

When she had told the story, her host commented:

"What you say is most singular. For it is an unhappy fact that Sir X. Y.'s youngest daughter, a beautiful girl, brought disgrace upon the family, was disowned and driven from home by her father, and died broken-hearted."[5]

Not all ghosts, it is pleasant to know, bring notification of impending or already consummated tragedy. Many seem to exist solely for the purpose of giving a warning of trouble which may be averted by taking proper precautions, and sometimes they are a direct means of preventing disaster. Thus, a guest at a Back Bay hotel in Boston was hurrying along a dimly lighted corridor to catch an elevator she thought she saw waiting for her, when unexpectedly the form of a man appeared at the entrance to the elevator. She was almost upon him, and stopped short in order to avoid a collision. At once he disappeared, and she then saw that although the door in the elevator shaft was wide open, the car was at the bottom of the shaft, into which she certainly would have fallen had not the phantasmal figure checked her onward rush.

Or take this instance, reported by Lady Eardley:

"One day I went to my bathroom, locked the door, undressed, and was just about to get into the bath, when I heard a voice say:

"'Unlock the door!'

"I was startled and looked around, but of course no one was there. I had stepped into the bath when I heard the voice twice more, saying:

"'Unlock the door!'

"On this I jumped out and did unlock the door, and then stepped into the bath again. As I got in I fainted away and fell down flat in the water. Fortunately, as I fell, I was just able to catch at a bell handle, which was attached to the wall above the tub. My pull brought the maid, who found me, she said, lying with my head

[5] Mrs. M.'s detailed account of this experience, with a corroboratory statement by Mr. M., is published in the Proceedings of the Society for Psychical Research, vol. viii, pp. 178-179.

under water. She picked me up and carried me out. If the door had been locked I would certainly have been drowned."

Still more impressive is an experience in the life of an Englishwoman named Mrs. Jean Gwynne Bettany. Her statement is corroborated by her father and mother.[6]

"On one occasion," she says, "I was walking in a country lane. I was reading geometry as I walked along, a subject little likely to produce fancies or morbid phenomena of any kind, when, in a moment, I saw a bedroom in my house known as the 'White Room,' and upon the floor lay my mother, to all appearance dead. The vision must have remained some minutes, during which time my real surroundings appeared to pale and die out; but as the vision faded, actual surroundings came back, at first dimly, and then clearly.

"I could not doubt that what I had seen was real, so, instead of going home, I went at once to the house of our medical man, and he immediately set out with me, on the way putting questions I could not answer, as my mother was to all appearance well when I left home.

"I led the doctor straight to the 'White Room,' where we found my mother actually lying as in my vision. This was true even to minute details. She had been seized suddenly by an attack at the heart, and would soon have breathed her last but for the doctor's timely advent."

Mrs. Bettany's father, Mr. S. G. Gwynne, adds:

"I distinctly remember being surprised by seeing my daughter, in company with the family doctor, outside the door of my residence; and I asked: 'Who is ill?' She replied: 'Mamma.' She led the way at once to the 'White Room,' where we found my wife lying in a swoon on the floor. It was when I asked when she had been taken ill that I found it must have been after my daughter had left the house. None of the servants in the house knew anything of the sudden illness, which our doctor assured me would have been fatal had he not arrived when he did."

In this last case, it should be noted the ghost seen was an apparition not of a dead person, but of a living one. This is most important, from the point of view of gaining insight into the nature and characteristics of ghosts.

The investigators who, a matter of twenty-five or thirty years ago, began for the first time to inquire into the subject in a scientific way, early made the interesting discovery that phantasms of the living are seen quite as frequently as phantasms of the dead. Besides which, it was found that ghosts could be produced experimentally—that by a mere act of willing, one person could make another, sometimes miles distant, see a ghost. Many successful experiments of the kind, supported by ample corroborative evidence, are now on record. For example:

Mr. B. F. Sinclair, at the time a resident of Lakewood, New Jersey, had occasion to go to New York to be absent several days. His wife was not feeling well when he left home, and he was greatly worried about her.

---

[6] See "Phantasms of the Living," vol. i, pp. 194-195.

"That night," to continue the narrative[7] in his own words, "before I went to bed, I thought I would try to find out, if possible, her condition. I had undressed, and was sitting on the edge of the bed, when I covered my face with my hands and willed myself in Lakewood at home, to see if I could see her. After a little, I seemed to be standing in her room before the bed, and saw her lying there, looking much better. I felt satisfied she was better, and so spent the week more comfortably regarding her condition.

"On Saturday I went home. When she saw me, she remarked:

"'I thought something had surely happened to you. I saw you standing in front of the bed the night you left, as plain as could be, and I have been worrying about you ever since.'

"After explaining my effort to find out her condition, everything became clear to her. She had seen me when I was trying to see her. I thought at the time I was going to see her and make her see me."

In at least one instance another experimenter, a German savant named Wesermann, performed the seemingly impossible feat of creating, by a simple act of volition, a ghost not of himself but of a person who was dead.

Herr Wesermann had been greatly troubled by the conduct of a friend, a young officer in the German army, and in the hope of reforming him, "willed" one evening that at eleven o'clock that night he should see in a dream an apparition of a lady in whom he had once been greatly interested, but who had been dead five years.

It chanced that at eleven o'clock, instead of being in bed and asleep, Herr Wesermann's friend was chatting with a brother officer. Nevertheless, the apparition came to him at the hour appointed, and was seen, not only by him, but by his companion also.

The door of his chamber seemed to open, and the ghost of his dead sweetheart walked in, "dressed in white, with black kerchief and bared head." Both officers started to their feet, and watched with bulging eyes while the ghost bowed gravely to them, turned, and without a word disappeared.

They followed instantly, rushing into the corridor, but saw only the sentry, who solemnly assured them that nobody but themselves had entered or left the room.[8]

Facts like these naturally raised in the minds of many of the investigators a belief that quite possibly ghosts could be explained without resorting to the alternative of dogmatically denying their reality or regarding them as supernatural beings. This belief was strengthened by other facts brought to light in the course of experiments to determine the actuality of telepathy, or thought transference as it used to be called.

---

[7] I quote from Mr. Sinclair's report to the Society for Psychical Research, and published by him in its Journal, vol. vii, p. 99.

[8] Herr Wesermann's experiments were reported by him in the Archiv für den Thierischen Magnetismus, vol. vi, pp. 136-139.

It was discovered that, under certain favoring conditions, thoughts could indeed be transmitted from mind to mind without passing through the ordinary known channels of communication; and furthermore that thoughts thus transmitted were often apprehended, not as mere ideas, but in the form of auditory or visual hallucinations.

Thus, if it were a question of "telepathing" the idea of a certain playing card, say the three of diamonds, the recipient, instead of simply getting the thought, "three of diamonds," might hear an hallucinatory voice saying to him, "three of diamonds," or might see three diamond-shaped objects floating before his eyes, the "ghosts" of three diamonds, so to speak.

Of even greater significance was the discovery that it frequently happened also that instead of getting the message which the experimenter had consciously attempted to send, the recipient would get other ideas merely latent in the experimenter's mind—ideas connected with his environment, something he had been doing, etc. Or the recipient might get the right message several hours after the experiment had been made—receiving it, for example, in a dream.

The obvious conclusion was that telepathy must be a function not of a person's ordinary consciousness, but of what psychologists call the subconsciousness, thus accounting for the difficulty of invariably obtaining satisfactory results in telepathic experiments.

In the light of these discoveries, then, the belief has been gaining ground that ghosts—real ghosts—are at most nothing but mental images impressed upon one mind by another through the subtle power of telepathy, and apprehended in the form of hallucinations of the various senses, just as any ordinary telepathic message may be apprehended.

A person is stricken with a mortal illness, is fatally injured, or is passing through some other great crisis likely to terminate in death. Consciously or subconsciously, he thinks of loved ones far away, and is seized with a longing to get into touch with them once more, if only to notify them of the catastrophe threatening him.

Across the intervening space, by what mechanism we as yet do not know, his thought wings its way to them, finds lodgment in their subconsciousness, and thence, when favoring conditions arise—as in some moment of mental relaxation—is projected into their consciousness before, at the time of, or after the sender's death, and is seen, or heard, it may be, as a Phantom Drummer, a Knocking Ghost, or the phantasmal image of the sender himself.

If, however, conditions are such as to prevent the message from emerging from the recipient's subconsciousness into his field of conscious vision, it may, on occasion, as telepathic experiments have proved, be retransmitted to a third party, and by him be apprehended; as, for example, the Drummer of Cortachy, in the two instances cited above, was heard not by members of the Ogilvy family, but by comparative strangers.

More than this, evidence has been accumulating to make it certain that in most cases not even telepathy is involved in the creation of ghosts, but that they are merely products of the seer's own subconsciousness. This was first clearly indicated by the results of an interesting "census of hallucinations," originated some years ago at the International Congress of Psychology, and simultaneously carried on—principally by members of the Society for Psychical Research—in the United States, England, France, Germany, and other countries. To thousands of persons the question was put:

"Have you ever, when believing yourself to be completely awake, had a vivid impression of seeing or being touched by a living being or inanimate object, or of hearing a voice, which impression, so far as you could discover, was not due to any external physical cause?"

Of the 27,339 replies received to this question[9] no fewer than 3,266 were in the affirmative. Many of those replying narrated true "ghost stories" similar to the ones given above; many testified to apparitions not of dead persons but of living friends; and in addition to this, the replies of many others brought out the interesting fact that there often were "ghosts" of inanimate objects—of hats and chairs and tables as well as of human beings.

One respondent, Mrs. Savile Lumley, testified that, in broad daylight and while taking a calisthenic lesson, she and another young woman "distinctly saw a chair over which we felt we must fall, and called out to each other to avoid it. But no chair was there."

The Reverend G. Lyon Turner, professor of philosophy at the Lancashire Independent College, Manchester, England, woke up one morning to find the ceiling of his room adorned with a huge chandelier of some ten arms, and the jets shining brightly through the ground-glass globes at the end of each arm. He knew that when he went to bed no chandelier had been there, and naturally feared that something was the matter with his eyesight.

"I moved my head," he said, "to see whether the phantom moved, too. But no, it remained fixed; and the objects behind and beyond it became more or less completely visible as I moved, exactly as would have been the case had it been a real chandelier. So I woke my wife, but she saw nothing."

Even more bizarre was the phantasm that appeared to another Englishman. Here is his own account of it:

"I had just gone to bed, and was—at least, this was my impression at the time—quite awake. The door of my room was ajar, and there was a light in the passage which half-illumined my room. Suddenly I became aware of a series of slight taps on the passage outside. These taps were not sufficiently loud for a human footstep; on the other hand, the volume of their sound was greater than that made by a walking-stick. I fully remember sitting up in bed and beholding two top-boots trot rapidly across the room and vanish into the opposite wall. The illusion was astonishingly vivid, and I can recall the details to this day. I have never had a waking dream since, and have never experienced ambulant top-boots except

[9] The detailed report of the results of this census will be found in the Proceedings of the Society for Psychical Research, vol. x, pp. 25-422.

on this occasion."

Whence the origin of these odd apparitions? The reply of modern science is that they were nothing more than the weird externalization of ideas latent in the minds of those perceiving them. Indeed, in the case of Mr. Turner there is absolute proof that this was the case, for that gentleman afterwards identified the phantom chandelier with one familiar to him as hanging from the ceiling of the college chapel in which he daily said prayers. Furthermore, there is proof—of which an abundance will be given in subsequent chapters—that often the ideas thus externalized relate to things once seen or heard but long since forgotten; it may be to things seen or heard in a wholly unconscious, or, rather, subconscious, way. And as with ideas of things, so with ideas of persons.

In this connection, as illuminating vividly the problem of ghosts, may well be given an experience narrated to me by Doctor Morton Prince, the eminent Boston psychopathologist, or medical psychologist.

A patient of his came to him one morning in a condition of extreme nervousness, declaring that the previous night she had seen a ghost. "I woke up," said she, "and saw at the foot of my bed a young woman, who gradually faded away." She maintained that at no time had she seen anybody resembling the apparition, but in the minute description she gave, Doctor Prince at once recognized a relative of his, with whom he remembered he had been talking in the hall when the patient last visited him. Saying nothing to her he quietly assembled a few photographs, and, before she departed, asked her to look them over.

"Why," she said, picking one up, "here is my ghost!"

"Yes," was Doctor Prince's reply, "and you saw your ghost in this house when you were here only a few days ago. I was talking to her as you came in."

"But," objected the patient, "I certainly did not see her, for I noticed somebody was with you, and I purposely turned away as I passed, lest I should seem rude."

"All the same," said Doctor Prince, "you saw her without being conscious of it—saw her, as it were, out of the corner of your eye. One fleeting glance would be enough to give you the memory image that you mistook for a ghost."

Undoubtedly Doctor Prince was right, and undoubtedly this dual law of subconscious perception and memory is enough to account for some of the most impressive ghosts cited in this chapter. Even the strange haunting of the Petit Trianon, as experienced by Miss Morison and Miss Lamont, may be said to find its explanation here.

It is true that both Miss Morison and Miss Lamont profess to have known little about the history of the Petit Trianon previous to their visit to Versailles. But their detailed report of the haunting contains statements showing that, subconsciously at any rate, they must have possessed considerable knowledge of the place. Miss Morison admits that she had, as a girl, great enthusiasm for Marie Antoinette, and had read not a little about her, including an article descriptive of her summer home; while Miss Lamont is a teacher of French history, and accordingly must have had rather more knowledge than the average person regarding the life story of Queen Marie. Besides which, and most significant, there was published, just before they went to Versailles, an illustrated magazine article picturing a historical fête in the gardens of the Petit Trianon, with some account of its history.

It is worth noting, too, that the two ladies were not haunted in exactly the same way, each of them seeing certain people and scenes that were not visible to the other. On the theory of a supernatural manifestation this would be hard to explain, but the difficulty vanishes if we recognize that the subconscious knowledge of the Trianon possessed by each must necessarily have differed.

The problem remains to account for the fact, as distinct from the facts, of the haunting. Why should Miss Morison and Miss Lamont, among all the thousands of visitors to the Petit Trianon, alone have had such an experience? To this, assuredly, there is no answer if one is going to stick to the old-fashioned notion of ghosts and attribute to them objective reality. But the answer is very simple on the modern scientific hypothesis.

Miss Morison and Miss Lamont, the psychologist would say, were haunted for the reason that, being of exceptionally romantic, impressionable temperaments, the ideas associated in their minds with the Petit Trianon, appealed to them with such "suggestive" force as to plunge them for the time being into a state of "psychical dissociation," during which their subconsciousness obtained complete control over the upper consciousness, and flooded them with its latent memories of all that they had ever read or heard about the place and its historic residents. In other words, they were as two persons "dreaming awake."

The same explanation would obviously apply to the ghostly vision seen on the lawn by Mrs. M. Nor do we need to go beyond the hypothesis of subconscious perception to account for the experiences of Lady Eardley and the guest at the Boston hotel. In the latter case it is necessary to assume nothing more than that the lady who saw the apparition at the elevator entrance perceived her danger without being aware of it, and subconsciously developed the hallucination that enabled her to avoid it.

As to the Eardley case, it is a well-established medical fact that some diseases, in their initial stages, cause organic changes too slight to be noticed by the sufferer's upper consciousness, but plainly perceptible to his subconsciousness which, through symbolical dreams or hallucinations, sometimes seeks to convey to the upper consciousness a warning that all is not well.

I myself have had such an experience. A number of years ago, beginning in the summer, I was troubled by a recurrent nightmare in which, although the details were not always the same, the central incident never varied. Always the nightmare ended with a phantom cat clawing viciously at my throat. I did not then know as much about dreams as I do now, so, beyond thinking vaguely that "it must mean something," I paid no attention to this repeated nightmare.

At the end of six months I had an attack of grippe, necessitating treatment by a throat specialist, who speedily discovered in my throat a growth of which I consciously had had no knowledge. With its removal the recurrent dream of the cat instantly ceased to trouble me.

Lady Eardley's case was, doubtless, quite similar, the only difference being that the subconscious warning was conveyed to her upper consciousness, not in dream, but as an auditory hallucination. And, in the somewhat parallel case of the ghost seen by Doctor Langtry, it seems a safe assumption that if the frightened clergyman had advised the child's father to place her under medical care at once, the subsequent fatality might have been averted.

In the Langtry case, however, there must have been operative also a telepathic factor. And since the telepathic explanation of ghosts is still the subject of much controversy, it will be well, before proceeding farther, to state exactly what is known to-day regarding telepathy.

CHAPTER II

WHY I BELIEVE IN TELEPATHY

SOME years ago, when living near New York, I had a curious dream that made a deep impression on me. In this dream I seemed to be at a club or hotel, when a messenger boy entered and announced that I was wanted up-stairs. There I found in a large room a family with whom I had been intimate in my boyhood in Canada. I had heard nothing of them for years, and naturally was delighted to see them. But I was struck with the absence of one of the sons, Archie, who, as a youngster of about my own age, had been one of my closest friends.

To my inquiry as to why he was not with them, I was told: "He's gone," a statement which, despite its vagueness, seemed in the dream a wholly adequate and satisfactory reply. When I awoke, however, with the dream details vividly in mind, I had a strong feeling that, as I said to my wife: "Something serious must have happened to Archie Tisdale." The sequel proved that this feeling was amply justified.

For it developed that, at about the time of my dream, he had died from an illness of which I knew nothing until, prompted by the dream, I made inquiries about him.

Again, many years earlier, whiling away the time one summer evening in a green lane that led to the shore of a beautiful Canadian lake, I had an experience which similarly gave me food for thought. I had been leaning on a rail fence, taking in the glories of the fading sunset. It was one of those evenings and one of those scenes of which poets delight to sing, and as I gazed across the lake at the changing hues on the distant hills, slowly turning from blue to gray as the twilight deepened, I gave myself up to the pleasurable day-dreaming so common in the romantic age of youth.

Suddenly I was roused by hearing my name called, in a tone so faint, albeit perfectly audible, that for a moment I could fancy the call came from beyond the lake. The next instant, however, I realized that it was what, with my larger psychological knowledge of to-day, I should term wholly subjective, coming from within me rather than from without; and at the same time I distinctly got the impression that it was connected in some way with accident or illness befalling a young lady in whom I was then much interested—the young lady, in fact, who afterwards became my wife.

It was in vain that I sought to dismiss this impression as a mere freak of the imagination. So insistent did it at last become that I returned to the house and hastily scribbled a note, stating what I had heard—or, rather, thought I had heard—and expressing the hope that all was well.

My letter had to go to a distant city, and it was therefore several days before an answer could arrive. I well remember how, in the interval, I fretted and worried. But by return mail a reassuring reply reached me. Only, most strangely, the writer added that late in the afternoon of the day on which I heard the hallucinatory call, she had been overcome by heat, and was for some hours thought to be in a serious condition.

Once again I heard the same weird inward calling of my name—this time at eleven o'clock on the night of a Fourth of July celebration, when I was lounging in a hammock on the bank of the Niagara River, watching the last of the fireworks on the American side. I was quite alone, as the friends with whom I was staying had retired an hour or more before; and, for that matter, it was not their custom to address me by my first name. Yet I heard myself called, faintly but distinctly, and seemingly from across the water, precisely as in my previous experience.

As in that experience, also, I instinctively associated the calling with my absent sweetheart, and wrote to her at once. Two days later, our letters crossing, I received word that on the night of the Fourth she had taken an overdose of headache powder, with consequences that might have been serious had not medical assistance been promptly obtained.

But even more singular than any of the foregoing is a happening connected with an accident that occurred to my wife while she was still a mere schoolgirl.

With a party of young people she had gone on an outing to a Maine lake resort, and in the dusk of a pleasant evening started for a drive in an old-fashioned hay-wagon. There was no thought of danger, and the drive was thoroughly enjoyed by all until, coming down a long and rather steep hill, the breeching broke, and the horses ran away. At a sharp turn in the road, half-way down the hill, the drive came to a sudden and disastrous end with the overturning of the wagon.

A number of its occupants were seriously hurt, my wife, with great presence of mind, saving herself by jumping clear of the wagon just as it began to go over. Even so, she did not escape uninjured, her face being badly cut.

Now comes the curious part of the affair. Early the next morning a telegram from her mother in Boston was handed to her. It read: "Are you hurt or ill? Wire at once. Am writing." The letter which followed gave the amazing information that the previous night—that is, the night of the accident—the mother had had an unusually vivid dream in which she saw her daughter driving in a carriage, thrown out of the carriage, and badly cut about the face. So realistic was the dream that on waking it frightened her, and led to the sending of the telegram.

Obviously the question arises: Were these four strange experiences representative merely of extraordinary chance coincidences, or were they indicative of the action of some direct means of communication from mind to mind by other than the ordinary recognized channels of communication?

Personally I am satisfied that chance alone will not suffice to account for them, and that they are veritable instances of the workings of a faculty latent in all mankind and operable in accordance with a true, if as yet little understood, law of nature—call it telepathy, thought transference, or what you will.

And in saying this, I am well aware that, even if my belief is in agreement with that entertained by many eminent men of science—such as Sir Oliver Lodge, Sir William Crookes, Camille Flammarion, Charles Richet, Theodore Flournoy, Henri Morselli, Professor W. F. Barrett and the late William James—it is contrary to the opinion held by the great majority of scientists at the present day. Their view, to put it briefly, is that there is no such thing as telepathy; that chance coincidence, deliberate or unconscious falsification, and errors of memory are sufficient to explain most instances of alleged telepathic communication; and that the remainder are reducible to the operation of more or less familiar principles in the psychology of the subconscious—notably the law of hyperæsthesia, or unusual extension of the senses of sight, hearing, smell, etc.

I am perfectly willing to admit that much which passes as telepathy may be thus reducible. For example, I am seated writing at the desk in my study. Unexpectedly there flashes into my mind an idea concerning a person of whom I have not thought for weeks or months. The next instant the doorbell rings, and presently the maid informs me that the very person of whom I have that moment been thinking has entered the house.

This is a not infrequent experience, as most of my readers will concede. So frequent is it that it is absurd to attempt to account for it on the hypothesis of chance coincidence. But neither would it be always safe to raise the theory of telepathy. For it might well happen that while I was seated intent on my work, with the study windows closed, my ear nevertheless caught the sound of footsteps coming down the street, or on my porch; that I subconsciously recognized in them my friend's walk, and that I consequently, though without knowing why, thought of him at that precise moment. This is assuredly a possible explanation—though I am far from conceding that in all such cases it is the only explanation properly applicable.

So, likewise, one must be constantly on guard against over-readily accepting as evidences of telepathic action the feats of "mind reading" often undertaken by way of parlor amusement. Stage "mind reading" by professional entertainers may be safely left out of the reckoning, as undoubtedly based on methods of conscious trickery and deceit. But in a private gathering, where there can be no question of confederates and deliberate signaling, surprising results are sometimes obtained in the finding of hidden objects, etc. On the surface this would seem explicable only on a telepathic basis, yet in reality it is commonly brought about by "muscle reading" rather than by true "mind reading."

Experiment has shown that the effort to concentrate thought on a given matter—a name or an object—tends to produce some form of muscular activity, either subconscious whispering of the name thought of, or subconscious movement in the direction of the object. If, as is the rule, the spectators are supposed to keep their minds fixed intently on the name or object they have selected for the "test," some of them are apt to give these involuntary muscular hints, which the performer will accept and act upon, it may be without being clearly conscious of the source of his information.

Still it must be added that experiments in the "willing game" have been carried out under conditions and with results indicating that occasionally, at all events, successes are achieved without any such subconscious guidance. Not so very long ago some interesting and most striking experiments of this sort were described to me by Professor J. H. Hyslop.

"The subject of my experiments," said he, "was a young woman of good family, who was credited with having exceptional ability in divining the thoughts and wishes of others. It was arranged that I should investigate her powers, and accordingly for a period of some weeks I had frequent sittings with her, in the presence of a few interested and trustworthy friends.

"The plan followed in every experiment was this: The young woman having left the room, I mentally selected some more or less complicated action for her to perform upon her return. I then wrote down on a slip of paper what I wished her to do, showed it to the others, and concealed it in a book, which did not leave my hand until after the completion of the experiment. From first to last not a word was spoken by any one, so as to guard against any possible hyperæsthesia of hearing on her part.

"The young woman was then called back, and almost invariably proceeded to execute the commands mentally given her. She did this so promptly that I cannot conceive how she could possibly have got any unconscious hints from those present, and conscious signaling was out of the question.

"For instance, I once wrote on my paper an order for her to pick out of a vase a bunch of keys I had hidden there, cross the room with the keys, and place them on the mantel-piece. She entered, stood for but a moment with her eyes closed, and then, swiftly passing to the vase, which was on the floor, picked up the keys, turned, and deposited them on the mantel-piece as I had mentally suggested. It was all done so quickly and spontaneously that to my mind it afforded strong evidential proof of true thought transference.

"She was not always successful, but some of her failures were quite as instructive as her successes. On three occasions she executed, not the commands I had written on the paper, but commands I had thought of writing but for one reason or another had abandoned. No one in the room excepting myself knew of these previous intentions, so she could have derived her knowledge of them from the involuntary movements of no one excepting me; and if it had actually been a matter of subconscious guidance, it is obvious that my muscular indications would have related not to the abandoned commands but to the commands I actually wished her to carry out.

"All things considered, my experiments with this young woman satisfy me that the hypothesis of subconscious guidance is not always properly applicable, even when the 'mind reader' is in a position to see or hear the persons testing him."

Assuming, however, for the sake of argument, that Professor Hyslop's conclusion is erroneous, and that the involuntary movement theory does always suffice as an explanatory hypothesis when experimenter and subject are in the same rooms, it becomes manifestly and hopelessly inadequate when applied to explain the transmission of ideas between persons a considerable distance apart. Yet what I consider abundant proof has been experimentally obtained that such transmission may, and sometimes does, take place—occasionally in most dramatic form.

Take, for example, the experience of a French lady, Mme. Clarence de Vaux-Royer, who, feeling uneasy one day about a friend who was then living in the United States, thought she would cable to him. Unfortunately it was Sunday, and her maid found the cable office closed. Mme. de Vaux-Royer then decided to attempt a telepathic experiment, and, knowing that her friend was mourning the death of his mother and of a favorite sister, decided to try and impress him with an idea that they were near him and would comfort him in any trial he might be undergoing. She told her maid of her intention, and asked the maid to note the date, so as to be able to give corroborative evidence if the experiment succeeded.

This was on November 7. Ten days later the American mail brought to Mme. de Vaux-Royer a letter from her absent friend, who, after referring to some matters of wholly private interest, stated:

"Last night (the 7th), while I was praying, I saw, hovering above my head, some gold circles, which gradually floated away until I could no longer see them. At the same time I seemed to hear some one calling to me: 'Mother! Mother! Sister Minnie!' Then the circles floated back, approaching until they almost touched my head. Oh, how much comfort I felt! How they inspired me with sentiments of goodness and happiness!"

From this it is manifestly only a step to the experimental production of telepathic phantasms of the human form, as in the two instances given in the previous chapter (the Wesermann and Sinclair experiments), and in numerous other instances, of which one or two additional may well be narrated here. In one, a Harvard professor, an acquaintance of Professor James, on whose authority I quote the story, having heard of the possibility of telepathic hallucinations, determined one evening that he would try to make an apparition of himself appear to a friend, a young lady who lived half a mile from his home. He did not mention his intention to her or to anybody else. The next day he received a letter, in which she said:

"Last night about ten o'clock I was in the dining-room at supper with B. Suddenly I thought I saw you looking in through the crack of the door at the end of the room, toward which I was looking. I said to B.: 'There is Blank, looking through the crack of the door!' B., whose back was toward the door, said: 'He can't be there. He would come right in.' However, I got up and looked in the other room, but there was nobody there. Now, what were you doing last night, at that time?"

At that precise moment, as he told Professor James, "Blank" had been at home, sitting alone in his room, and trying "whether I could project my astral body to the presence of A."

Possibly had the young lady been alone, and not actively engaged, she might have had a more definite view of the phantasm of her absent friend, for experience has shown that solitude and quiet are favoring conditions for the perception of telepathic apparitions. In nearly every instance reported to the Society for Psychical Research the percipient of the phantasm is alone and in a more or less passive, quiescent frame of mind. Such a condition usually obtains immediately before or immediately after sleep, and it is then that experimental apparitions are seen most plainly. Though occasionally they are vividly experienced when the percipient is in a state of the most active consciousness, as in the following case, reported by the agent—that is, the person sending the telepathic message—and confirmed by the percipient, an English clergyman now dead, the Reverend W. Stainton Moses.

"One evening," runs the agent's account, "I resolved to try to appear to Z., at some miles distance. I did not inform him beforehand of the intended experiment; but retired to rest shortly before midnight with thoughts intently fixed on Z., with whose rooms and surroundings, however, I was quite unacquainted. I soon fell asleep, and awoke next morning unconscious of anything having taken place. On seeing Z. a few days afterward, I inquired:

"'Did anything happen at your rooms on Saturday night?'

"'Yes,' replied he, 'a great deal happened. I had been sitting over the fire with M., smoking and chatting. About twelve-thirty he rose to leave, and I let him out myself. I returned to the fire to finish my pipe, when I saw you sitting in the chair just vacated by him.

"'I looked intently at you, and then took up a newspaper to assure myself I was not dreaming, but on laying it down I saw you still there. While I gazed without speaking, you faded away.'"

Of course in the case of all single experiments like these,[10] the skeptically inclined might plausibly fall back on the theory of chance coincidence. But it is impossible seriously to entertain this hypothesis in cases where experiments in the telepathic transmission of ideas have been carried on repeatedly and with an astonishing measure of success.

To mention only the most notable experiments of this systematic kind, I would call attention to the results obtained by two sets of English investigators, the first comprising two ladies named Clarissa Miles and Hermione Ramsden, the second two gentlemen, F. R. Burt and F. L. Usher. As I see it, indeed, the Miles-Ramsden and Burt-Usher experiments have the additional interest that they not only make clear some of the fundamental laws of genuine thought transference, but also show just why it is that we can never hope to obtain such absolute control of the telepathic process as to be able to send mental messages from one to another with the same ease and certainty as we now send ordinary telegrams and marconigrams.

This inability of control has long been a stock objection against belief in telepathy, especially among the scientifically trained. "Not until we can repeat at will, and with invariable success, the experiment of direct transference of thought, will we accept telepathy as established," say these scientific skeptics. "We know that

[10] Accounts of other experiments of the same type will be found in my book, "The Riddle of Personality," pp. 140-142.

if, in our chemical and physical laboratories, we bring such and such elements together, such and such action will always follow. We must be able to do as much with telepathy before we will accept it." But the Miles-Ramsden and Burt-Usher experiments show that there are excellent reasons for affirming that telepathy is a fact, and that nevertheless its processes cannot be governed with the certitude possible in the case of chemical and physical processes. There are factors involved which elude, and must always elude, the directive control of the experimenter.

In the experiments by the Misses Miles and Ramsden it was arranged that, at a stated hour of a stated evening in each week, Miss Ramsden—who acted throughout as the percipient, or receiver of the telepathic messages—was to remain for a few minutes in a condition of complete passivity, and immediately afterwards was to note on a post-card whatever ideas came into her mind during that time. The post-card was then to be mailed to Miss Miles, who, for her part, was to think of Miss Ramsden at intervals during the day agreed on, and in the evening was to make a post-card entry—to be mailed to her friend forthwith—of the idea or ideas she had tried to convey to her telepathically. Thus, in the event of achieving any degree of success, they would have a perfect documentary record to substantiate their claims.

As to the distance separating them, it ranged from a few score to several hundred miles. They made, in fact, three distinct series of experiments, with about a year's interval between each series. During the first they were at their homes, Miss Miles in London, Miss Ramsden in Buckinghamshire. During the second, Miss Ramsden was in Inverness, in northern Scotland, and Miss Miles visiting friends in various parts of England. The third series was carried on while Miss Miles was making a tour of the beautiful Ardennes region of France and Belgium, Miss Ramsden at the same time being again in the Scottish Highlands.

Thus there was a progressive increase in the distance between them for each series, but this seems to have made no difference in the result. In each, as the attested record shows, Miss Ramsden succeeded in getting, completely or in part, no fewer than two out of every five of the messages her co-experimenter tried to "telepath" to her. Such a proportion is clearly too high to be explained away on the theory of chance coincidence, and this theory is rendered still more untenable by the attendant circumstances which the record reveals.

On one occasion Miss Miles, who is an artist, had been busy in the afternoon painting a model's hands. She thought of this when evening came, and determined to endeavor to impress Miss Ramsden with the idea "hands". In her post-card, written at seven o'clock the same evening, Miss Ramsden stated that of several ideas which had come into her mind at the experiment-hour the "most vivid" was "a little black hand, quite small, much smaller than a child's, well formed, and the fingers straight. This was the chief thing.

Similarly, having noticed at a meeting in London a curious pair of spectacles worn by a gentleman seated near her, Miss Miles, on returning home in the early evening, wrote down the word "spectacles," with the idea of "telepathing" it to Miss Ramsden. The latter's post-card entry for that evening noted that "spectacles" was "the only idea that came to me after waiting a long time."

Again, while on a sketching expedition to an English village, Miss Miles was much amused by an adventure with a large white pig. She selected this pig as the subject of her next telepathic communication, the result of which Miss Ramsden, writing as almost always on the night of the experiment, thus reported:

"You were out of doors rather late, a cold, raw evening, near a railway station; there was a pig with a long snout, and some village children. It was getting dark."

On the other hand, in several instances Miss Ramsden's impressions contained much which Miss Miles had not consciously sought to convey to her. And this brings us to what is unquestionably the most important feature of the experiments.

As was said, about two out of every five messages were correctly received, in whole or in part. But it frequently happened in the case of the seeming failures, that while Miss Ramsden did not get the ideas which Miss Miles was endeavoring to send to her, she did get ideas relating to people, things and events much in Miss Miles's mind at that moment, or which had been more or less in her mind during the day of the experiment.

To illustrate, Miss Miles once tried to make Miss Ramsden think of "pussies, or cats." What Miss Ramsden did think of was "a manuscript, pinned by a patent fastener in one corner." And, oddly enough, Miss Miles had spent a good part of that afternoon reading to a friend from a manuscript "fastened together," as the friend has testified, "with a patent fastener." Similarly, during Miss Miles's visit to the English village above mentioned, Miss Ramsden's report for one experiment ran:

"First I saw dimly a house, but I think that you wish me to see a little girl with brown hair down her back, tied with a ribbon in the usual way. She is sitting at a table with her back turned and seems very busy indeed. I think she is cutting out scraps with a pair of scissors. She has on a white pinafore, and I should guess her age to be between eight and twelve."

Miss Miles had not been trying to make Miss Ramsden think of anything of the sort. But the description fitted perfectly her landlady's little daughter, of whom the mother, Mrs. Laura Lovegrove, says:

"I have a little girl aged eleven, with brown hair, tied with a ribbon in the usual way. She wears a pinafore, and, being ill, often amuses herself cutting out scraps."

Another time, when the hour for the experiment arrived, Miss Miles forgot all about it, being busy writing letters to some friends. In particular she was absorbed in framing an answer to an important letter from a Polish artist, written in a peculiar script. Miss Ramsden's report for that evening was:

"I felt that you were not thinking of me, but were reading a letter in a sort of half-German writing. The letters have very long tails to them. Is there any truth in that?"[11]

[11] The experiments of the Misses Miles and Ramsden are reported in detail in the Proceedings of the Society for Psychical Research, vol. xxi, and in the Journal of the Society

Significant also is the fact that precisely the same sort of thing occurred in the more recent experiments between Mr. Burt and Mr. Usher, who, like Miss Miles and Miss Ramsden, conducted their investigations in a careful, methodical, conscientious way, and over a long period of time.

Mr. Usher, like Miss Miles, invariably acted as the sender of the telepathic communications, while Mr. Burt was the percipient. From first to last the latter remained in London, while Mr. Usher was part of the time in Bristol, more than one hundred miles from London, and part of the time in the Austrian city of Prague, a thousand miles away. On each experiment-evening it was Mr. Usher's practice, at the hour previously agreed upon, to sit alone in a dimly lighted room, draw some design on a piece of paper, and remain for fifteen minutes thinking intently of the design and "willing" to transmit it to Mr. Burt, who, at the same hour, would be seated in a darkened room in London, noting the images that passed before his mind's eye, and, at the expiration of fifteen minutes, setting down on paper the one or two that had seemed to him most vivid.

Nearly fifty experiments were thus made, with results defying any explanation by the theory of chance coincidence. And, as in the Miles-Ramsden experiments—for the matter of that, as also in Professor Hyslop's experiments—it at times happened that when Mr. Burt totally failed to draw a design corresponding with that which Mr. Usher had drawn, Mr. Burt's design did correspond with images demonstrably in Mr. Usher's mind at or immediately before the moment of the experiment.

Thus, one evening in Prague Mr. Usher tried to make Mr. Burt get the impression of an oblong composed of numerous small dots. Instead Mr. Burt saw and designed a peculiar plume-like ornamentation, which Mr. Usher instantly recognized as a picture of part of the unusual carving on the table at which he had been seated. On another occasion—the eighteenth experiment—Mr. Usher sought to transmit a crude design of a flower in a pot. What Mr. Burt actually drew was an excellent representation of a lighted cigarette with the smoke curling away from it.

"And," says Mr. Usher, "the evening that he drew this was the first evening I had smoked a cigarette while experimenting with him."

Such incidents, with those cited in connection with the experiments of Professor Hyslop and the Misses Miles and Ramsden, in my opinion go to show exactly why it is that one cannot hope to obtain unfailing control over the process of telepathy. For they indicate that at bottom genuine thought transference depends not so much on conscious *willing* as on subconscious *feeling*. It is not necessarily the things about which one thinks most strongly, but rather things which are tinged with some emotional coloring, that are most likely to become subjects of telepathic communication.

And these experiments further indicate that, on the receiver's part also, the mechanism involved in the transmission of telepathic messages belongs rather to the subconscious than to the conscious portion of the mind. In order to allow the

---

for Psychical Research, vol. viii. The report of the Burt-Usher experiments appears in the Annales des Sciences Psychiques, January and February, 1910.

emergence of the transmitted ideas into the field of conscious knowledge, there seems to be always necessary some form of psychical "dissociation"—as in a trance, dream, reverie, or moment of absentmindedness. Such states of dissociation are not always easy to bring about voluntarily; and when they are brought about, whether voluntarily or involuntarily, it by no means follows that ideas received telepathically will forthwith and rapidly rise above the threshold of consciousness.

For, as recent psychological experiment and observation have shown, in dissociated states the tendency is for the emergence chiefly of ideas which, through their emotional associations, are of deep personal significance—as when we dream of persons or things associated with events that once affected us profoundly. Every one of us has subconscious reminiscences of this sort, and with these personal subconscious reminiscences any ideas which have been transmitted telepathically have of necessity to compete for emergence. They may get through or they may not; whether they will get through apparently depends in large measure on the degree of their own emotional intensity.

Hence it is that that scientist is doomed to perpetual unbelief who boasts that he will never place credence in telepathy until he can play with it as he plays with the chemicals in his test tubes. One cannot handle feelings as one can handle a chemical compound, nor can one manipulate at will the subconscious as though it were a physical substance. Hence, too, the case for telepathy must always rest less on experimental evidence—strong though the Miles-Ramsden and Burt-Usher experiments demonstrate that this sometimes is—than on well-authenticated instances of spontaneous occurrence, which have been recorded in ever-increasing volume since systematic investigation of the subject was first undertaken a scant quarter of a century ago.

In such instances, the records further show, one of the commonest forms in which the telepathic message is received is that of an auditory hallucination, as in the "voice" heard by me on the shore of the Canadian lake and on the bank of Niagara River. When there is connected with the sending of the message some supreme crisis in the career of the sender—the crisis, it may be, of the moment of death—the auditory hallucination is sometimes of such a nature as to make its dire meaning almost self-evident. In this respect I know of nothing more striking than a strange case reported, with ample corroborative evidence, to the Society for Psychical Research.

The narrator, a well-to-do Englishman, was living at the time in a country house. It was early spring, and on the night of his telepathic experience there had been a slight snowfall, just sufficient to make the ground white. After dinner he spent the evening writing until ten o'clock, when, to continue the story in his own words:

"I got up and left the room, taking a lamp from the hall table, and placing it on a small table standing in a recess of the window in the breakfast-room. The curtains were not drawn across the window. I had just taken down from the nearest bookcase a volume of 'Macgillivray's British Birds' for reference, and was in the act of reading the passage, the book held close to the lamp, and my shoulder touching the window shutter, and in a position when almost the slightest sound would be heard, when I distinctly heard the front gate opened and shut again with a clap, and footsteps advancing at a run up the drive; when opposite the window the steps changed from sharp and distinct on gravel to dull and less clear on the grass-slip below the window, and at the same time I was conscious that some one or something stood close to me outside, only the thin shutter and a sheet of glass dividing us.

"I could hear the quick, panting, labored breathing of the messenger, or whatever it was, as if trying to recover breath before speaking. Had he been attracted by the light through the shutter? Suddenly, like a gunshot, inside, outside, and all around, there broke out the most appalling shriek—a prolonged wail of horror, which seemed to freeze the blood. It was not a single shriek, but more prolonged, commencing in a high key, and then less and less, wailing away toward the north, and becoming weaker and weaker as it receded in sobbing pulsations of intense agony.

"Of my fright and horror I can say nothing—increased tenfold when I walked into the dining-room and found my wife sitting quietly at her work close to the window, in the same line and distant only ten or twelve feet from the corresponding window in the breakfast-room. *She had heard nothing.* I could see that at once; and from the position in which she was sitting, I knew she could not have failed to hear any noise outside and any footsteps on the ground. Perceiving I was alarmed about something, she asked:

"'What is the matter?'

"'Only some one outside,' I said.

"'Then, why do you not go out and see? You always do when you hear any unusual noise.'

"'There is something queer and dreadful about this noise,' I replied. 'I dare not face it.'"

Nothing more was heard, and early next morning he made a careful search in the grounds around the house, but not a footprint was to be seen in the snow, which had ceased falling long before the occurrence of the wailing cry. A little later in the day, however, word arrived that at ten o'clock the previous night one of his tenants, who lived half a mile distant and with whom he had spent the afternoon, had committed suicide by drinking prussic acid.

He had gone up to his bedroom, his groom testified at the inquest, had mixed the poison in a tumbler of water, drank it off, and, with a terrible scream, fell dead on the floor.

Fortunately, telepathic hallucinations do not usually come with such intensity or in such an alarming form. Often they are mere vague impressions that something unpleasant or disastrous is occurring to a relative or friend, and, as in the case of self-originating hallucinations like that reported by Lady Eardley, they occasionally impel to action that averts disaster. It was thus, to give a single instance, in an experience reported[12] by William Blakeway, a Staffordshire Englishman:

"I was in my usual place at chapel one Sunday afternoon, when all at once I thought I must go home. Seemingly against my will, I took my hat. When reaching the chapel gates I felt an impulse that I must hasten home as quick as possible, and I ran with all my might without stopping to take breath. Meeting a friend who asked why I hurried so, I passed him almost without notice.

"When I reached home I found the house full of smoke, and my little boy, three years old, all on fire, alone in the house. I at once tore the burning clothes from off him, and was just in time to save his life. It has always been a mystery to me, as no person whispered a word to me, and no one knew anything about the fire till after I made the alarm at home, which was more than a quarter of a mile from the chapel."

Here the wholly subconscious nature of the phenomenon, on the percipient's part at all events, is plainly evident. It is even more evident in all cases where, as frequently occurs, the telepathic message is received in a dream like that which was recorded in the opening paragraphs of this chapter. As is to be expected, too, in telepathic dreams we often find an element of symbolism. The news of illness, of accident, of death, or whatever it may be, is not conveyed directly, but indirectly, amid a mass of more or less relevant details of dream imagery.

A couple of years ago I received a letter from a lady living in Brooklyn, describing an experience that admirably illustrates this point. Her dream, however, was of such an intimate character that the names of the persons and places must be suppressed. Five years ago, this lady writes, her daughter became interested in a young man, Mr. V., whose suit, however, the mother discouraged. Afterwards her daughter met, fell in love with, and was happily married to a physician in the Government service. She soon went abroad with her husband, to a remote and isolated post. My informant continues:

"We could not hear from them all winter because they were ice-bound, but my thoughts of them were always most delightful, for their last letters were bubbling over with happiness, and I was lovingly busy getting things ready for them.

"Mr. V. had almost passed from my mind, when one morning, in the middle of June, I arose, took a bath, and, having a half-hour to spare, went back to bed again, falling into a deep sleep.

"Suddenly Mr. V. appeared to me in one of my lower rooms. It seemed to be breakfast time, and I invited him to have some. He accepted, and we sat together for some time, but I do not remember any of our conversation. Suddenly he arose, faced me, and, looking straight into my eyes, said emphatically:

"'Now she is mine! Nothing you can do will ever separate us again! This time she will belong to me!'

"I awoke with a start, much frightened. Then, realizing the situation, I thanked Heaven she was safely married, and promptly put the dream from me. This was about eight o'clock. At ten a despatch reached me saying that my daughter's hus-

[12] In "Phantasms of the Living," vol. ii, pp. 377-378.

band had died, from the result of a boating accident two weeks before."

Or, when apprehended in dream, the telepathic message may be so distorted that its true meaning cannot possibly be recognized immediately. A characteristic case of this kind occurred at the time of President Lincoln's assassination, though it is only recently that it was for the first time reported in detail by Mrs. E. H. Hughes, daughter of the San Francisco architect, S. C. Bugbee. It should be explained that before removing to California from Massachusetts in 1863, the Bugbees were well acquainted with the Booth family, and that John Wilkes Booth was an especial favorite of Mrs. Bugbee's. Says Mrs. Hughes, in her report to the American Institute for Scientific Research:[13]

"One night my mother woke my father suddenly, saying: 'Oh, Charles! I have had such a terrible dream! I dreamed that John Wilkes Booth shot me! It seemed that he sent me seats for a private box in a theater, and I took some young ladies with me. Between the acts he came to me, and asked me how I liked the play. I exclaimed, "Why, John Booth! I am surprised that you could put such a questionable play upon the stage. I am mortified to think that I have brought young ladies to see it." At that he raised a pistol, and shot me in the back of the neck. It seems as if I felt a pain there now.' After a while my mother fell asleep, and dreamed the same thing a second time.

"The next morning came the terrible news which plunged the nation into grief and mourning. Almost at the hour of my mother's dream, President Lincoln was assassinated; shot, in the back of the neck, in a private box at a theater, by John Wilkes Booth."

On the other hand, there may be no symbolism or distortion, the dream corresponding so realistically with the event as to make its significance manifest. To give an illustration, Mrs. Morris Griffith, an Englishwoman, reports:

"On the night of Saturday, the eleventh of March, I awoke in much alarm, having seen my eldest son, then at St. Paul de Loanda on the southwest coast of Africa, looking dreadfully ill and emaciated, and I heard his voice distinctly calling to me. I was so disturbed I could not sleep again, but every time I closed my eyes the appearance recurred, and his voice sounded distinctly, calling me 'Mamma!' I felt greatly depressed all through the next day, which was Sunday, but I did not mention it to my husband, as he was an invalid, and I feared to disturb him. Strange to say, he also suffered from intense low spirits all day, and we were both unable to take dinner, he rising from the table, saying: 'I don't care what it costs, I must have the boy back,' alluding to his eldest son.

"I mentioned my dream and the bad night I had had to two or three friends, but begged that they would say nothing of it to Mr. Griffith. The next day a letter arrived, containing some photos of my son, saying he had had fever, but was better, and hoped immediately to leave for a much more healthy station. We heard no more till the ninth of May, when a letter arrived with the news of our son's death from a fresh attack of fever, on the night of the eleventh of March, and adding that

[13] Journal of the American Society for Psychical Research, vol. iv, pp. 210-217.

just before his death he kept calling repeatedly for me."[14]

It is only a short transition from such a dream as this to a waking hallucination in which—as in the cases of experimental occurrence mentioned above, and those other cases detailed in the preceding chapter—phantom forms are discerned at the moment when the person seen is threatened by some danger or is passing through the supreme crisis of death.

But now, accepting telepathy as an established fact, the problem remains: How are we to explain it? What is the mechanism by which one person is able to transmit messages directly and instantaneously to another person although they may be half the world apart?

To this question, it must frankly be admitted, no positive answer can as yet be returned. But some extremely plausible hypotheses have been advanced, not by mere theorists but by eminent men of science, who, themselves affirming the actuality of telepathy, have given much thought to the problem of its mode of operation.

Sir William Crookes, for example, calling attention to the marvelous but undisputed facts of ethereal vibration as evidenced by the phenomena of wireless telegraphy and the Röntgen rays, urges that here we have quite possibly an adequate explanation of the mystery of telepathy on a wholly naturalistic basis—that is to say, a basis which enables us to accept telepathy without dislocating our entire conception of the physical universe.

"It seems to me," he suggests, "that in these rays [Röntgen rays] we may have a possible way of transmitting intelligence which, with a few reasonable postulates, may supply the key to much that is obscure in psychical research. Let it be assumed that these rays, or rays of even higher frequency, can pass into the brain and act on some nervous center there. Let it be conceived that the brain contains a center which uses these rays as the vocal chords use sound vibrations (both being under the command of intelligence), and sends them out, with the velocity of light, to impinge on the receiving ganglion of another brain. In this same way the phenomena of telepathy, and the transmission of intelligence from one sensitive to another through long distances, seem to come into the domain of law and can be grasped."[15]

This undoubtedly is the explanation that most strongly commends itself to those scientists who courageously acknowledge their belief in telepathy. Nor do they see any objection to it in the fact that people apparently are affected by the telepathic impulse only at certain times. For the brain of both sender and receiver may conceivably, on the analogy of wireless telegraphy, be set to transmit and receive telepathic communications only when attuned to vibrations of a certain amplitude. There is, however, as Sir William Crookes himself has recognized, another and really formidable objection to this vibratory hypothesis.

It is found in the fact that, assuming telepathic messages to be conveyed by a system of infinitely minute waves in the ether, we logically have also to assume

[14] "Phantasms of the Living," vol. i, pp. 343-344.

[15] Presidential Address to the Society for Psychical Research, January 29, 1897.

that these waves would still obey what is known as the law of inverse squares. By this is meant that, spreading on every side in ever-expanding waves, they would lose power in proportion to the square of the distance from their source. Consequently, it would not only require a tremendous initial energy to project them any great distance, but the farther they were sent the feebler they would become, so that in the case of a percipient remote from the agent, either the telepathic message would not be received at all or at most it would be received in exceedingly attenuated fashion. Whereas the fact is that, according to the results of such experimentation as that which I have described, complete failure often occurs when the experimenters are only a few yards apart, and brilliant successes are sometimes achieved at distances of hundreds of miles.

This consideration has led some thinkers—notably Sir Oliver Lodge, Professor W. F. Barrett, and the late F. W. H. Myers—to abandon outright all attempt at an explanation on a naturalistic basis, and to advance instead the view that telepathy is not explicable in physical terms because it is a wholly psychical process—"a direct and supersensuous communion of mind with mind." After all, though, as Mr. Frank Podmore has pointed out, this view rests simply on a negation—our present inability to conceive a thoroughly satisfactory explanation; and at any time scientific research may remove that inability, as has happened again and again in the past in the case of other and seemingly equally inexplicable phenomena.

Meanwhile, all that we, scientists and laymen alike, need do, is to remember that inability to explain gives us of itself no warrant to deny. We must acquaint ourselves with the facts before accepting or rejecting them. And for myself I can only say that the actuality of telepathy has to my mind been absolutely proved. With Sir Oliver Lodge:

"I am prepared to confess that the weight of testimony is sufficient to satisfy my own mind that such things do undoubtedly occur; that the distance between England and India is no barrier to the sympathetic communication of intelligence in some way of which we are at present ignorant; that just as a signaling-key in London causes a telegraphic instrument to respond instantaneously in Teheran—which is an everyday occurrence—so the danger or death of a distant child, or brother, or husband, may be signaled without wire or telegraph clerk, to the heart of a human being fitted to be the recipient of such a message."

CHAPTER III

CLAIRVOYANCE AND CRYSTAL-GAZING

THE word clairvoyance has acquired a decidedly sinister meaning in most people's minds. It is associated with professional spiritistic mediums, who lay claim to supernatural powers which they are ready, at a moment's notice, to exercise for all who are credulous enough to pay the fee they demand. Newspapers throughout the country daily contain advertisements of clairvoyants of this type, arrant humbugs, most of them, but often able, through cunningly acquiring information regarding their "sitters'" lives and family relationships, to persuade their victims that while "entranced" they are actually in contact with the "spirit world." Repeated exposures of their fraudulent methods have not driven them out of business, but have inspired a widespread and healthy distrust of their pretensions.

Nevertheless, it would be rash to conclude, as many of us do, that there is no such thing as genuine clairvoyance, by which is meant the ability to perceive distant scenes and events as if one were bodily present at the place of their occurrence. That such a faculty exists, although usable only on rare occasions, and that there is nothing in the least supernatural about it, are facts definitely established by the scientifically trained investigators who have been diligently attacking this and other psychical problems the past twenty-five years. Their researches have made it evident that in order to explain genuine clairvoyant phenomena it is not necessary to postulate the intervention of "spirits," or the flight through space of the clairvoyant's "astral body." At most, clairvoyance is simply a special form of telepathy, differing in degree but not in kind from the phenomena discussed in the preceding chapter.

There is absolutely no evidence to justify the hypothesis of so-called "independent clairvoyance," advocated by occultists of every shade of spiritistic belief, and utilized by unscrupulous tricksters to dazzle the imagination of their dupes. On the other hand, as I hope to make convincingly clear, there is plenty of proof that the scenes which the true clairvoyant perceives, and is frequently able to describe with graphic detail, are in reality only mental images, visual hallucinations, developed by the same process that enables any ordinary telepathic message to be apprehended.

It must be acknowledged, however, that the telepathic connection is sometimes extremely difficult to trace; as, for example, in the few indisputable instances, reported by Professor James and other trustworthy investigators, in which the services of clairvoyants have been successfully invoked to find the bodies of persons drowned or otherwise accidentally killed under circumstances seemingly precluding any one from having knowledge of the place or manner of their death.

A typical case of the kind occurred a few years ago in connection with the mysterious death of a New Hampshire girl, Miss Bertha Huse, of Enfield, who was drowned in Mascoma Lake.

For three days after the disappearance of Miss Huse, one hundred and fifty of her townspeople searched vainly for her. She had last been seen alive on a long bridge crossing the lake, and it was supposed that she had fallen from it or had deliberately committed suicide. The waters were dragged but without result, and failure also attended the efforts of a professional diver from Boston employed by a sympathetic citizen.

Meantime, in the little town of Lebanon, some miles distant, a Mrs. Titus fell into a trance, during which she talked to her husband and described to him a spot in the lake where she said the body of the Huse girl was lying. So strongly was Mr. Titus impressed by her statements that, next day, he took her to Enfield, where the diver, following her instructions, quickly found the body in the place located by her.

Mrs. Titus afterwards gave other, if less sensational, demonstrations of a similar character; and Professor James, who made a close study of her case, publicly stated his belief that her experiences form "a decidedly solid document in favor of the admission of a supernormal faculty of seership—whatever preciser meaning may later come to be attached to such a phrase."

There are also on record certain well-attested dreams presenting the same difficulty of identifying the agent, or sender, of the clairvoyant vision. A characteristic dream of this sort is reported by Mrs. Alfred Wedgwood, daughter-in-law of the English savant, Hensleigh Wedgwood.

"I spent the Christmas holidays with my father-in-law in Queen Anne Street," says Mrs. Wedgwood,[16] "and in the beginning of January I had a remarkably vivid dream, which I told to him next morning at breakfast.

"I dreamed I went to a strange house, standing at the corner of a street. When I reached the top of the stairs I noticed a window opposite with a little colored glass, short muslin blinds running on a brass rod. The top of the ceiling had a window veiled by colored muslin. There were two small shrubs on a little table. The drawing-room had a bow window, with the same blinds; the library had a polished floor, with the same blinds.

"As I was going to a child's party at a cousin's, whose house I had never seen, I told my father-in-law I thought that that would prove to be the house.

"On January tenth I went with my little boy to the party, and, by mistake, gave the driver a wrong number. When he stopped at number twenty, I had misgivings about the house, and remarked to the cabman that it was not a corner house. The servant could not tell me where Mrs. H. lived, and had not a blue-book. Then I

[16] Proceedings of the Society for Psychical Research, vol. vii, pp. 47-48.

thought of my dream, and, as a last resource, I walked down the street, looking up for the peculiar blinds I had observed in my dream. These I met with at number fifty, a corner house, and, knocking at the door, was relieved to find that it was the house of which I was in search.

"On going up-stairs, the room and windows corresponded with what I had seen in my dream, and the same little shrubs in their pots were standing on the landing. The window in which I had seen the colored glass was hidden by the blind being down, but I learned on inquiry that it was really there."

In this case the dream, though devoid of any dramatic feature, served a useful purpose, as did a much more spectacular dream occurring to Doctor A. K. Young, an Irish magistrate and land-owner.[17] In his dream he suddenly found himself standing at the gate of a friend's park, many miles from home. Near by were a group of persons, one a woman with a basket on her arm, the rest men, four of whom were tenants of his own, while the others were unknown to him. Some of the strangers seemed to be making a murderous attack on one of his tenants, and he ran to his rescue.

"I struck violently at the man on my left," he says, "and then with greater violence at the man to my right. Finding to my surprise that I did not knock either of them down, I struck again and again, with all the violence of a man frenzied at the sight of my poor friend's murder. To my great amazement, I saw that my arms, although visible to my eye, were without substance; and the bodies of the men I struck at and my own came close together after each blow through the shadowy arms I struck with. My blows were delivered with more extreme violence than I think I ever exerted; but I became painfully convinced of my incompetency. I have no consciousness of what happened, after this feeling of unsubstantiality came upon me."

Next morning Doctor Young awoke feeling stiff and sore, and his wife informed him that he had greatly alarmed her during the night by striking out "as if fighting for his life." He then told her of his curious dream, and asked her to remember the names of the actors in it recognized by him. The following day he received a letter from his land agent stating that the tenant whom he had dreamed he saw attacked had been found unconscious, and apparently dying, at the very spot where Doctor Young had in his dream tried to defend him; and that there was no clue to his assailants.

That night Doctor Young started for the scene of the tragedy, and immediately upon his arrival applied to the local magistrate for warrants for the arrest of the three men whom, besides the injured tenant, he had recognized in the vision. All three, when arrested and questioned separately, told the same story, confirming the details of the dream, even to the incident of the presence of the woman with the basket. They had said nothing about the affair because they were afraid it would make trouble for them, but they denied any complicity in it, asserting that while walking home with them between eleven and twelve at night, the tenant—who, by

[17] The evidence relating to this dream will be found in "Phantasms of the Living," vol. i, pp. 381-383.

the way, ultimately recovered—had been attacked by a couple of strangers, whose companions had prevented them from interfering to protect him.

According to Mrs. Young, it was between eleven and twelve o'clock on the night of the fight that her sleeping husband had frightened her by his violent actions.

Here the telepathic impulse causing the clairvoyant dream may have come either from the injured tenant himself or from one of the three spectators known to Doctor Young. The difficulty is to conceive an adequate reason for any of them thinking of him, even subconsciously. But, granting for argument's sake the possibility of independent clairvoyance, the still more thorny question at once arises why his "astral body" should have chosen to journey to that precise spot at that precise moment.

The obstacles in the way of such a conception as independent clairvoyance are too serious to be overcome. Nor is it necessary to resort to it, in view of the fact that in the vast majority of clairvoyant cases it is possible to establish definitely the telepathic association.

Here, by way of illustration, is a typical case, fully as impressive as Doctor Young's, but leaving no doubt as to its origin. It was reported to the Society for Psychical Research by Mrs. Hilda West, daughter of Sir John Crowe, who was at the time British consul general for Norway.

"My father and brother," runs Mrs. West's narrative, "were on a journey during the winter. I was expecting them home, without knowing the exact day of their return. I had gone to bed at the usual time, about eleven P. M. Some time in the night I had a vivid dream, which made a great impression on me.

"I dreamed I was looking out of a window, when I saw father driving in a Spids sledge, followed in another by my brother. They had to pass a cross-road, on which another traveler was driving very fast, also in a sledge with one horse. Father seemed to drive on without observing the other fellow, who would, without fail, have driven over father if he had not made his horse rear, so that I saw my father drive under the hoofs of the horse. Every moment I expected the horse would fall down and crush him. I cried out 'Father! Father!' and woke in a great fright.

"The next morning my father and brother returned. I said to them: 'I am so glad to see you arrive quite safely, as I had such a dreadful dream about you last night.' My brother said: 'You could not have been in greater fright about him than I was.' And then he related to me what had happened, which tallied exactly with my dream. My brother in his fright, when he saw the feet of the horse over father's head, called out: 'Oh, father! Father!'"

Compare with this the very similar instance of clairvoyance in a waking or semi-waking state, experienced by Mrs. Helen Avery Robinson, of Anchorage, Kentucky, and communicated by her, with a corroborative letter from her son, to Professor Hyslop:

"My son and a friend had driven across the country to dine and spend the evening with friends. The rest of the household had retired for the night. I was awakened by the telephone, and looked at the clock, finding it eleven-thirty. I knew my son would soon be in, and thought of a window down-stairs, which I felt might not have been locked, and I determined to remain awake and ask my son to make sure it was secure.

"As I lay waiting and listening for him, I suddenly saw their vehicle, a light break-cart, turn over, my son jump out, land on his feet, run to the struggling horse's head, his friend hold on to the lines, and in a moment it was gone and I knew all was right and felt no disturbance.

"I met my son as he came in, and spoke of the window. He said: 'We tipped over, mother.' I replied: 'Yes, I know it. I saw you.' And described what I saw, which he said was just as it happened. I did not see them before they started out, as his friend called for him with his horse and vehicle, so I did not know in what style they went."

It should be added that the spot where the cart was overturned was so far from the Robinson house that, even had it been broad daylight, Mrs. Robinson could not possibly have witnessed the accident from her bedroom.

In the same way a young man named Frederic Marks, in Wallingford, Connecticut, clairvoyantly—and most dramatically—beheld an accident occurring to his brother, Charles, on Oneida Lake, in New York State, hundreds of miles from Wallingford.[18] Charles Marks and a friend, Arthur Bloom, had gone for a sail on the lake, were caught in a storm, and almost wrecked through the giving way of their boom. Charles, however, springing into the bow, managed to make the boom fast again, and they succeeded in running to shore.

It was when their danger was greatest that they were seen clairvoyantly by Frederic Marks, who, it being a rainy afternoon in Wallingford, was lounging in his room.

"I do not think I fell asleep," he testifies, "nor did I seem fully awake. But all at once I seemed to be facing a severe storm of wind and rain. As I looked into the storm a small boat with a sail came, driven helplessly along through a seething, boiling mass of water. Two young men were in it, one trying to steer and control the boat, the other apparently trying to dip out water and work on the sail.

"One of the two, in a moment of greatest peril, tried to tear down the sail from its mast. The face of my brother came clearly into view, with an expression on it that remains with me now. The boat righted and sped on. I saw a low shore that it was driving toward. The boat grew fainter as it neared the shore, and consciousness came back to me, and, whatever it was, whether a dream or a vision, passed away."

Fortunately, young Marks did not keep his singular experience to himself, but hastened down-stairs and told his employer—a Mr. Bristol, with whom he was living—of what he had seen. He was laughed at, of course, and assured that it was "only a dream." But three or four days afterward a letter arrived from Charles

[18] The evidence relating to this case is published in the Proceedings of the Society for Psychical Research, vol. vii, pp. 359-364.

Marks, bringing unexpected verification of his brother's story.

Even more detailed, in point of clairvoyant perception of a distant scene, is the strange dream of a physician, Doctor C. Golinski, of Krementchug, Russia. It was Doctor Golinski's custom to take a nap during the day, and one afternoon he lay down on a sofa as usual, about half-past three. While asleep, he says:[19]

"I dreamed that the doorbell rang, and that I had the usual rather disagreeable sensation that I must get up and go to some sick person. Then I found myself transported directly into a little room with dark hangings. To the right of the door leading into the room is a chest of drawers, and on this I see a little paraffin lamp of a special pattern. To the left of the door I see a bed, on which lies a woman suffering from severe hemorrhage. I do not know how I come to know that she has a hemorrhage, but I know it. I examine her, but rather to satisfy my conscience than for any other reason, as I know beforehand how things are, although no one speaks to me. Afterward I dream vaguely of medical assistance which I give, and then I awake."

It was then half-past four. About ten minutes later the doorbell rang, and Doctor Golinski was summoned to a patient. His surprise may be imagined when he found that he was ushered into the identical room of his dream. So astonished was he that he immediately approached the bed on which his patient was lying, and said to her:

"You are suffering from a hemorrhage."

"Yes," was her reply, in a tone of great astonishment. "But how do you know it?"

She then told him, in answer to his questions, that the hemorrhage had set in about one o'clock, but had not been severe enough to alarm her until between three and four; and that it was not until nearly half-past four that she had decided to send for him.

Nearly every instance of spontaneous clairvoyance that is sufficiently authenticated to compel credence, resembles these cases, and the similarity between them and cases of ordinary telepathic hallucination, as described in the chapter on telepathy, is too striking, it seems to me, to leave any doubt regarding their true nature. The only points of difference are that there is a greater amount of detail in clairvoyant visions, and that the percipient often experiences a sensation of being actually present at the scene beheld. But this latter fact is easily comprehensible when we remember that the same sensation of "otherplaceness" is often experienced in dreams that have no clairvoyant significance, and experienced with an equal feeling of reality, dissipated only when the dreamer awakes. As to the greater amount of detail, it is only necessary to assume that in clairvoyant cases the telepathic action is intensified by some favoring condition in the percipient's mind, just as some non-clairvoyant dreams are more detailed and vivid than others.

Besides which, the telepathic basis of clairvoyance has been experimentally demonstrated. One of the investigators for the Society for Psychical Research, Mr.

[19] Proceedings of the Society for Psychical Research, vol. vii, pp. 39-41.

G. A. Smith, once hypnotized a lady and requested her to "look into" the business office of a friend of his and tell him what she saw there. Much to his surprise she immediately began to describe the office with great exactness, although he was positive she had never visited it.

It then occurred to him that possibly she was acquiring her knowledge of it by telepathy from his own mind, and to test this theory he thought of an imaginary umbrella, which he pictured to himself as lying open on his friend's writing table. In a minute or so, the clairvoyant uttered a cry of astonishment, and exclaimed:

"Why, how strange! There's a large umbrella open on the table!"

Usually, however, experiments like this fail, the entranced clairvoyant being able to discriminate between the thoughts which correspond to reality and those which are wholly imaginary. But that the process involved in clairvoyance is unquestionably telepathic has been otherwise proved by the fact that when conditions are imposed on clairvoyants absolutely excluding the possibility of thought transference from one mind to another, they are conspicuously unsuccessful in their efforts to obtain results. If, as often happens, they are able to describe distant places which they have never seen but with which other persons are necessarily familiar, they are nevertheless unable to state, for example, the number on a bank note, chosen at random from among others and placed in their hands in a sealed box without anybody previously ascertaining just what the number is.

Such a test, if successful, would be decisive proof of independent clairvoyance; but I have yet to learn of any clairvoyant who has been able to meet it, although the effort has been frequently made. It should be pointed out that, in order to give it evidential value, there must not be the slightest possibility of any one even glancing at the bank note before it is put into the sealed box; for, as has already been said, it is now known that the eye is far keener than we usually realize, and that the merest glance may often put us in possession of facts which, sinking into the memory, may afterward emerge to astonish and perhaps mystify us. Once they were lodged in the mind, a clairvoyant could, of course, obtain these facts from us telepathically, and thus achieve a seeming success even in the bank note or some similar test.

Indeed, this power of subconscious perception is of itself sufficient to explain many undoubtedly genuine instances of clairvoyance. There is obviously no need to go beyond it to account for such a clairvoyant dream as the following, reported by a lady who has declined to allow her name to be published:

"A number of years ago I was invited to visit a friend who lived at a large and beautiful country seat on the Hudson. Shortly after my arrival I started, with a number of other guests, to make a tour of the very extensive grounds. We walked for an hour or more, and thoroughly explored the place. Upon my return to the house, I discovered that I had lost a gold cuff-stud, which I valued for association's sake. I merely remembered that I wore it when we started out, and did not think of or notice it again until my return, when it was missing. As it was quite dark, it seemed useless to search for it, especially as it was the season of autumn and the ground was covered with dead leaves.

"That night I dreamed that I saw a withered grapevine clinging to a wall, and with a pile of dead leaves at its base. Underneath the leaves, in my dream, I distinctly saw my stud gleaming. The following morning I asked the friends with whom I had been walking the previous afternoon if they remembered seeing any such wall and vine, as I did not. They replied that they could not recall anything answering the description. I did not tell them why I asked, as I felt somewhat ashamed of the dream; but, during the morning, I made some excuse to go out on the grounds alone. I walked hither and thither, and, after a long time, I suddenly came upon the wall and vine exactly as they looked in my dream.

"I had not the slightest recollection of seeing them, or passing by them on the previous day. The dead leaves at the base were lying heaped up, as in my dream. I approached cautiously, feeling rather uncomfortable and decidedly silly, and pushed them aside. I had scattered a large number of the leaves when a gleam of gold struck my eye, and there lay the stud, exactly as in my dream."[20]

Akin to this is an exceptionally interesting case that was reported to me by a young lady attending college at Greeley, Colorado. Her father, it appears, had sent her a check, which for a day or two she delayed cashing. Then, being without money, she looked for it in the place where she supposed she had put it, but, to her dismay, discovered that it was not there. A thorough search of her room failed to bring it to light, and, as it was not a personal check of her father's, she was greatly worried, thinking that it might be impossible to duplicate it.

A couple of nights later she had a curious dream in which she saw herself standing in front of a bookcase in the college library. On a certain shelf were five books, one bound in blue, another in yellow, and between them three with a white binding. She took down one of the white-covered volumes, opened it idly, and in the middle of the book found her check.

Next morning she awoke with no memory of the dream, nor did she recall it when, later in the day, she visited the college library and came across this identical placing of books. It recurred to her only when she glanced into one of the white-covered volumes. Feeling rather "foolish," and also not a little apprehensive, she took down a second volume of the same set, opened it, and there, sure enough, was the missing check!

She then remembered that the book in which it was found had been in her room for some hours the day she received her father's letter. What happened, I have no doubt, was that she absentmindedly slipped the check into the book, and then, so far as her upper consciousness was concerned, forgot all about it. But subconsciously she would remember and subconsciously would be reminded of it the day before the dream when, in the college library, she happened to see the same book again, without, perchance, any conscious knowledge of seeing it. That night, in sleep, her mind busied itself once more with the problem of the missing check, this time to good purpose.

Very similar is a dream for which I am indebted to Mr. Andrew Lang, who got it from the dreamer, an English lawyer. This gentleman had sat up late to write

[20] Proceedings of the American Society for Psychical Research, vol. i, pp. 361-362.

letters, and about half-past twelve went out to post them. On his return he missed a check for a large amount received by him during the day. He searched everywhere in vain, went to bed, and soon fell asleep. Then he dreamed that he saw the check curled around an area railing not far from his own door. Waking, he was so impressed that, although it was not yet daylight, he got up, dressed, walked out of the house, and found the check at the spot indicated by his dream.

In another case a Californian, visiting in Sullivan County, New York, lost a gold ring given him by his sister. That night he dreamed he saw it lying in the sand beneath a swing, in which he had been sitting in the afternoon. It was actually there, as he ascertained by looking next day. Similarly, a clerk in a customs house recovered a valuable document, the loss of which would have cost him his position. And the wife of a clergyman, the Reverend W. F. Brand, of Emmorton, Maryland, had revealed to her in a dream the hiding-place of a sum of money which, six months before, she had put away at her husband's request, but had afterward accidentally slipped into a bundle of shawls.

Decidedly, we not only see more than we are aware of, but we also remember more and for a far longer time than is usually supposed.

Which brings me to another point of great importance to the student of clairvoyance and other psychical problems, and also, as will appear in a later chapter, of tremendous significance in affairs of everyday life. The tenacity of memory is such that nothing one sees is really forgotten. It merely slips, as it were, into some subterranean region of the mind, whence, days and months and even years afterward, it may be recalled. Of this we have incontrovertible proof in the phenomena of crystal-gazing, a species of clairvoyance in which, by gazing into a crystal or a glass of water, or any small body with a reflecting surface, it is sometimes possible to perceive hallucinatory pictures of people and places situated far beyond the gazer's normal field of vision, and occasionally depicting events occurring at the moment they are seen in the crystal.

Occultists, as will readily be understood, set great store by crystal-gazing, finding in it positive proof of spirit action. But again it is unnecessary, even in the most extraordinary instances recorded, to adopt any other explanatory hypothesis than that of telepathy, and in most cases the source of the visions can be traced directly to latent memories in the gazer's own mind.

This has been beautifully demonstrated by Miss Goodrich-Freer, a lady who developed the faculty of crystal-gazing for the express purpose of studying and analyzing its hallucinatory images. Not everybody, I should perhaps say, can attain the degree of mental passivity requisite to seeing pictures in the crystal, but fortunately for the cause of scientific progress, Miss Goodrich-Freer was eminently successful.

With the aid of her crystal, Miss Goodrich-Freer has frequently recalled dates and other information which she had forgotten and wished to remember; and on at least one occasion, under exceptionally peculiar circumstances, she was enabled to supply an address which was of no special interest to her, but was of special interest to a relative. Here is her own account of the episode:[21]

"A relative of mine was talking one day with a caller in the room next to that in which I was reading, and beyond wishing that they were *farther*, I paid no attention to anything they said, and certainly could have declared positively that I did not hear a word. Next day I saw in a polished mahogany table, '1, Earl's Square, Notting Hill.' I had no idea whose this address might be; but some days later my relative remarked: 'H. (the caller aforesaid) has left Kensington. She told me her address the other day, but I did not write it down.' It occurred to me to ask: 'Was it, 1, Earl's Square?' And this turned out to be the case."

On another occasion, she says in the long report she has made on the subject to the Society for Psychical Research, she saw in the crystal the picture of a dark-colored wall, covered with white jessamine. She had been taking a walk that morning through the streets of London, and she thought that perhaps the crystal image represented some spot she had passed in her walk, though this seemed unlikely, both because she could not remember having seen such a wall, and because jessamine-covered walls are by no means common in London streets. But the next day she retraced her steps, and presently came to the identical scene of her crystal vision, the sight of it bringing the immediate recollection that at the moment she passed this spot the day before she had been engaged in absorbing conversation with a friend, and her attention was wholly preoccupied. The fact, however, of its reproduction in the crystal made it evident that, by the subtle power of subconscious perception she had obtained a perfect mental image of it.

Similarly, while busied one day with household accounts, she opened the drawer of her writing table to get her bank-book, and her hand came in contact with her crystal. Welcoming the suggestion of a change in occupation, she took it up, and began to gaze into it. But, she says:

"Figures were still uppermost, and the crystal had nothing more attractive to show me than the combination seven-six-nine-four. Dismissing this as probably the number of the cab I had driven in that day, or a chance grouping of the figures with which I had been occupied, I laid aside the crystal and took up my bank-book, which I certainly had not seen for some months, and found, to my surprise, that the number on the cover was 7694. Had I wished to recall the figures, I should, without doubt, have failed, and could not even have guessed at the number of digits or the value of the first figure."

It is not surprising to find Miss Goodrich-Freer adding:

"Certainly, one result of crystal-gazing is to teach one to abjure the verb 'to forget' in all its moods and tenses."

Still it is possible that in the act of opening the drawer, she caught a glimpse, without realizing it, of the number on the bank-book. There are many cases, though, in her experience and in the experience of other crystal-gazers, proving absolutely that latent memories dating back even to childhood may be thus recalled; and similar evidence is forthcoming from hallucinations experienced without the aid of a crystal. A "psychic" with whom Professor Hyslop has often experimented,

[21] In the Proceedings of the Society for Psychical Research, vol. viii, p. 489.

and whose home is in Brooklyn, used to have a recurrent visual hallucination of a bright blue sky overhead, a garden with a high fence, and a peculiar chain pump in the garden, situated at the back of the house.

Some time later she left Brooklyn to pay a visit to her girlhood home in Ohio, where she met a lady who invited her to tea. After tea they went into the garden, and there, to her amazement, she saw the high fence and the chain pump of her hallucination. She felt quite sure that she had never been in the place until that day, and it looked very much as though she had been given a supernatural revelation of it. But the mystery was solved on her return to Brooklyn.

Telling her mother of her odd experience, she asked if she thought there was any possibility she could have visited that particular house and garden in her younger days.

"Why, yes," was the unexpected reply. "When you were a little girl, two or three years old, I often took you to it."

But not all crystal visions may thus be attributed to the emergence of subconscious perceptions or the recrudescence of forgotten memories. There are some in which the telepathic action of mind upon mind is clearly manifested, and in which the crystal seems to serve as a mechanical aid, enabling the percipient to become aware of the telepathic message. In no case, however, as I have already said, is it necessary to go beyond telepathy to find an adequate explanation.

The same applies to the still more singular phenomena to which we shall turn next—the phenomena of automatic speaking and writing, regarded by many as affording incontrovertible proof of the validity of the spiritistic belief that the dead can and do communicate with the living.

CHAPTER IV

AUTOMATIC SPEAKING AND WRITING

THERE is a widespread belief that spiritism—or spiritualism, as it is more commonly known—is on the wane, and will soon be relegated to the limbo of extinct religions. But the facts indicate otherwise. At a conservative estimate, there are to-day, in the United States alone, no fewer than 75,000 avowed spiritists, in more or less regular attendance at the meetings of nearly 450 spiritist societies, and possessing church property valued at $2,000,000; and more than 1,500,000 believers who, without openly identifying themselves with any society, accept the ministrations of 1,500 public and 10,000 private mediums. Spiritism has even "followed the flag" into the Philippines, séances being held at Manila and elsewhere.

This certainly is a remarkable showing for a moribund religion, and what makes it more remarkable is the fact that spiritism, from its very beginnings sixty years ago, has been permeated with fraud. Its founders, the Fox sisters, daughters of a New York farmer, were naughty little girls who amused themselves by making strange noises which superstitious persons interpreted as communications from the dead. This proving profitable to the sisters Fox, the business of producing "spirit knockings" spread from town to town, and forthwith modern spiritism was born. Since then its record has been a long and dismal catalogue of swindles exposed by skeptical investigators. Scarcely a month passes without a story of some sensational exposé; yet, disproving all predictions to the contrary, spiritism continues to expand, constantly welcoming new recruits to its ranks.

Several reasons account for its amazing progress under what would appear to be the most adverse conditions imaginable. One is the innate tendency of many people to dabble with the occult and mysterious. Another is the appeal spiritism makes to the most sacred emotions of humanity. Its central doctrine is that it is possible for the dead to communicate with their surviving relatives and friends, through the mediumship of "psychics" gifted with extraordinary powers. Thus the hope is raised that messages of good cheer may be received from loved ones who have passed to the great Beyond—that their voices may be heard, their faces seen, and their hands clasped by those from whom death has separated them.

To the spiritistic séance, consequently, go grief-stricken men and women, skeptical perhaps, but fervently hopeful that their skepticism will be overcome. To borrow Professor James's striking phrase, they are already deeply imbued with "the will to believe," and are in no mood for close observation of what happens in the séance room. Usually, to speak plainly, they are utterly lacking in the qualities that make a scientific investigator. The sense of their loss is all-absorbing, and in this state of mind it is easy for any trickster who poses as a medium to delude them into fancying that they have actually been in touch with the dead.

But the main reason why spiritism has survived repeated exposés, and persists as a force to be reckoned with in the religious life of to-day, is the fact that it is by no means altogether synonymous with swindling. There are certain phenomena, particularly so-called automatic speaking and writing, which it is out of the question to attribute invariably to trickery and deceit. While one need have no hesitation in dismissing as fraudulent[22] all "physical" mediums—that is to say, mediums whose stock in trade is the production of such phenomena as the "materialization" of spirit forms and faces, the levitation and flinging about of furniture, and the striking of the "sitters" by unseen hands—the case of the automatists, or "psychical" mediums, is decidedly different.

These are mediums who, after passing into a peculiar condition of trance, and occasionally while seemingly in their usual waking state, appear to be controlled by some outside intelligence, and, when so controlled, utter or write information which it is hard, if not impossible, to believe they could have obtained by any ordinary means. To be sure, there is a host of spurious automatists, against whom one cannot be too watchfully on guard. Some of these are out and out cheats, as brazen as the most rascally materializers. Some depend for their success on guessing and on inferences shrewdly drawn from hints unconsciously dropped by their patrons. Quite a number, however, undoubtedly seem to exercise a gift not possessed—or, at all events, not utilized—by everyday men and women.

One Sunday evening, in the late nineties, I visited the spiritist church on Bedford Avenue, Brooklyn, of which the late Ira Moore Corliss was then pastor. In his day Mr. Corliss was probably the most prominent medium in Brooklyn, a city where spiritism has always flourished. He was an obviously religious-minded man, and one who sincerely believed that it was his mission to act as an intermediary between this world and the next. That evening the usual order of services in spiritist churches was followed—a prayer, some hymn singing, a sermon, or "inspirational discourse," and, lastly, the giving of "test messages," in which the medium passed rapidly up and down the aisles, pausing here and there to deliver oral communications alleged to come from the world of spirits.

Seated next to me was an elderly gentleman of dignified appearance, who watched the proceedings with a quiet smile of contempt. It was evident that this was the first time he had ever seen anything of the kind, and that he was both amused and disgusted. Suddenly Mr. Corliss, halting directly in front of him, said, in the quick, nervous way common to him when under "spirit control":

"I have a message for you, sir."

"For me?" repeated the elderly gentleman, incredulously.

"Yes, sir, for you. There is a spirit here that wants to thank you for your kindly

[22] Of course, strictly speaking, the term "fraudulent" should not be applied to those mediums who are the victims of a peculiar form of hysteria. This is discussed in detail in the next chapter.

thought of him to-day. It is the spirit of a rather tall man, heavily built, clean-shaven, with bright, tender eyes. He says his name is Henry Ward Beecher."

The smile faded from the other's face. He bent forward, listening intently.

"Go on," he said.

"This spirit," continued the medium, "says that he is glad to know you have not forgotten him. He says that he was with you this afternoon, when you went to the cemetery and took this flower from his grave."

With a dramatic gesture Mr. Corliss drew from the lapel of his astonished auditor's coat a sprig of geranium, and held it up so that all could see it.

"Am I not right?" he demanded.

"You are. Quite right."

Afterward I joined the elderly gentleman on the sidewalk, and plied him with questions. I found him greatly mystified.

"This is too much for me," said he. "I am a stranger to Brooklyn, and had never attended a spiritualist meeting until to-night. I only dropped in out of curiosity. But it is true that this afternoon I visited the cemetery where Henry Ward Beecher is buried, and picked this flower from near his grave, as a memento of my visit. Mr. Beecher was a very good friend to me in my younger days. How the medium could know these facts I cannot imagine. I had told nobody of my trip to the cemetery, and I am positive that no one saw me pick the flower."

On another occasion I took an artist friend to the first séance he ever attended. The medium was a psychic of the Corliss type, an automatist who delivered his "spirit messages" by word of mouth. There were perhaps a dozen other sitters present. To one of these, a thin, gaunt, haggard-looking young woman, the entranced medium announced the presence of "a spirit named Wagner." It was none other, it appeared, than the spirit of the great musician, who promised he would aid her with her musical compositions. A smile of infinite content transformed her careworn features, as she leaned over and whispered to my friend:

"The spirit of Liszt is already helping me. With Wagner's aid I cannot fail."

One could not smile in face of the story of boundless faith and pitiful struggle these few words told. And with the next sitter pathos rose to positive tragedy.

"There is the spirit of a man here, whose name is Frederick," the medium declared, "and he comes to you, madam. Take my hand."

Slowly a woman, dressed in deep mourning, stood up and extended her hand. Intensity was written in every line of her face.

"There were two Fredericks," she said. "Which is it?"

"It is the Frederick—it is the Frederick, who, while on earth, did this."

And he struck her sharply on the arm. Tears filled her eyes.

"I understand," she murmured, "I understand. What does he say?"

All this was interesting, but not convincing. For aught we could tell to the contrary, the medium had familiarized himself with the life stories of these women, who doubtless were regular attendants at his séances. But now he passed to the friend by my side.

"A message for you, sir," said he, "from the spirit of a military-looking man. Yes, he says that when he was in this sphere he was a commander of soldiers, a general. This is what he looks like."

He launched into a long description, which I could see was making a profound impression on my friend.

"Has he anything particular to say to me?" he asked.

"He says that you must on no account decline the offer that has been made to you to go West—that you will never regret going."

Less than two hours earlier my companion had told me of a commission unexpectedly tendered him, involving a long sojourn in California. At the medium's words he turned pale, and glanced around as though half expecting to see a ghost standing behind his chair.

When the séance had come to an end, and we were walking home together, he solemnly assured me that the medium had accurately described a dead friend, an army officer of the rank of general, whose advice, had he been alive, he would have sought with regard to his projected journey to California.

Again, there is an interesting case reported from New England by the Reverend Willis M. Cleaveland. Among Mr. Cleaveland's parishioners was a young woman, Miss Edith Wright, who developed mediumistic abilities, being controlled at times by what purported to be a discarnate spirit. Dreading notoriety, Miss Wright gave very few séances, and then only to her closest friends or to sitters with whom her friends were well acquainted, and in whose discretion they could place reliance.

One of these was Mr. Cleaveland, who, being interested in psychical research, undertook to obtain, if possible, proof of the identity of the supposed communicating spirit. If you really are a spirit, he said in effect, you ought to be able to give us some facts about yourself, something about your history while you were on earth, with data that will enable us to obtain confirmation of what you say. The "control" readily conceded the reasonableness of this, and in the course of several séances made twenty-six personal statements, of which the most significant were:

That her name was Amelia B. Norton.

That she had been the daughter of an orthodox clergyman, of the "water type."

That she had lived near the Kennebec River, in the State of Maine.

That when writing letters it had been her custom to sign herself by the initials N. N., meaning Nellie Norton.

That she had died in middle life.

That when quite young she had had a love affair with a Mr. L. C. Brown, who was still living and engaged in business in Boston, at an address which the "spirit" gave.

As goes without saying, Mr. Cleaveland at once wrote to Mr. Brown, and in a few days received a reply from him, in which he said:

"I was out in the town of Sharon very recently, and called on an elderly gentleman who was a manufacturer there when I resided there as a boy in my teens. To my surprise, as we were reviving old recollections of fifty years ago, he spoke of a Miss Norton that he said I was sweet on at that time.

"The facts of the case are that Mary B. Norton, who always signed herself Nellie B. Norton, came there, a young miss about my age. We were, I guess, ardent lovers, but in the course of two years I left the town and she did, and I knew very little of her for a few years after that. I think it was about five years later that on my way home from the White Mountains I stopped off at her home in Maine, which was beside a large river. I feel sure this was the Kennebec River. Her father was an orthodox minister, but I do not understand the meaning of the 'water type.' I think some two years later she was residing in Fairhaven and sent me some papers that contained letters written by Mary B. Norton, but from that time—some over forty years—I have not seen her. I heard that she died some years ago, and think she must have been about fifty years of age."

Later Mr. Brown wrote again, saying that on second thought he was not certain that her name might not have been Amelia instead of Mary, as he had always known her "only as Nellie B."[23]

It is to the constant occurrence of incidents like these that the vitality of spiritism is mainly due. To many people it seems impossible to account for such detailed and abundantly corroborated proofs of personal identity on any hypothesis short of actual spirit control. Yet in the last analysis, when viewed in the sober light of latter-day scientific knowledge of the workings of the human mind, it will be found that they do not afford the conclusive demonstration of the validity of the spiritistic doctrine which on the surface they appear to yield. For there is always the possibility—amounting, I feel warranted in saying, to certainty—that what they really indicate is not communication with the dead, but thought transference between living minds.

In fact the telepathic connection between the mind of the medium and the mind of the sitter is often most obvious. Take the three cases just cited, and which are typical of mediumistic communications. The statements made by the medium Corliss to the friend of Henry Ward Beecher were statements relating to an incident fresh in the latter's memory, and therefore easily obtainable by the telepathic process, which, there is reason to believe, is exceptionally at the command of genuine psychics. Likewise, my artist friend was much occupied mentally with the problems involved in the California offer, and was doubtless thinking of it, consciously or subconsciously, at the time the medium invoked the "spirit" of the army officer whose advice my friend would have sought had that officer still been in the flesh. All the medium had to do was to tap telepathically my friend's subconsciousness and extract from it every detail of the "revelation" so sensationally

[23] This case is reported in detail in the Proceedings of the American Society for Psychical Research, vol. ii, pp. 119-138.

made to him in the séance room.

Slightly different, however, is the case of Miss Edith Wright. Here the facts thought to emanate from the dead Amelia B. Norton were facts concerning which Miss Wright's sitter, the Reverend Mr. Cleaveland, was ignorant. But it is most significant that, continuing his researches, Mr. Cleaveland made the discovery that Miss Norton's old sweetheart, Mr. Brown, had had at least one sitting with Miss Wright. Mr. Brown denied that he had ever said anything about Miss Norton in Miss Wright's presence; but his memory may have played him false, and, in any event, she could have got from him by telepathy the data with which she afterward astonished both him and Mr. Cleaveland. Let me remind the reader that among the few definitely ascertained laws of telepathy is the fact that it is possible for telepathic messages to lie long latent in the recipient's mind before emerging above the threshold of consciousness.

This is of even greater significance in connection with the rarer, but still quite numerous, instances in which the mediumistic communications offered as evidence of spirit identity refer to incidents not known by the medium or by the sitter or by any previous sitter. These, spiritists insist, are absolutely inexplicable on the telepathic basis. I can make their position clearer by citing an illustrative case taken from the experience of that greatest of automatists, the New England medium, Mrs. Leonora E. Piper, whose remarkable mediumistic faculty was first made known to the scientific world by Professor James thirty years ago, and who has since been repeatedly investigated by leading members of the Society for Psychical Research. Detectives have been employed to dog her footsteps, open her mail, watch her every move. But not once have they detected her in fraudulent practices; and, on the other hand, she has given such convincing proof of the genuineness of her power that some of the most skeptical among her investigators have ended by accepting at face value her "messages from the dead."

On one occasion, while she was being investigated in England by a committee of experts, that famous English psychical researcher, Sir Oliver Lodge, placed in her hands, while she was entranced, a gold watch once the property of an uncle of his who had died some twenty years before. It was now owned by another uncle, a twin brother of the dead man.

"I was told almost immediately," says Sir Oliver, "that it had belonged to one of my uncles—one that had been very fond of Uncle Robert, the name of the survivor—that the watch was now in the possession of this same Uncle Robert, with whom its late owner was anxious to communicate. After some difficulty and many wrong attempts, Doctor Phinuit—a 'spirit' alleged to be controlling Mrs. Piper—caught the name Jerry, short for Jeremiah, and said emphatically, as if impersonating him: 'This is my watch, and Robert is my brother, and I am here. Uncle Jerry, my watch.'

"All this at the first sitting on the very morning the watch had arrived by post, no one but myself and a shorthand clerk, who happened to have been introduced for the first time at this sitting by me, and whose antecedents were well known to me, being present.

"Having thus ostensibly got into communication through some means or other with what purported to be Uncle Jerry, whom I had indeed known slightly in his later years of blindness, but of whose early life I knew nothing, I pointed out to him that to make Uncle Robert aware of his presence it would be well to recall trivial details of their boyhood, all of which I would faithfully report.

"He quite caught the idea, and proceeded during several successive sittings ostensibly to instruct Doctor Phinuit to mention a number of little things such as would enable his brother to recognize him. References to his blindness, illness, and main facts of his life were comparatively useless from my point of view; but these details of boyhood, two-thirds of a century ago, were utterly and entirely out of my ken.

"'Uncle Jerry' recalled episodes such as swimming the creek when they were boys together, and running some risk of getting drowned; killing a cat in Smith's field; the possession of a small rifle, and of a long, peculiar skin, like a snakeskin, which he thought was now in the possession of Uncle Robert.

"All these facts have been more or less completely verified. But the interesting thing is that his twin brother, from whom I got the watch and with whom I was thus in correspondence, could not remember them all. He recollected something about swimming the creek, though he himself had merely looked on. He had a distinct recollection of having had the snakeskin, and of the box in which it was kept, though he did not know where it was then. But he altogether denied killing the cat, and could not recall Smith's field.

"His memory, however, was decidedly failing him, and he was good enough to write to another brother, Frank, living in Cornwall, an old sea captain, and ask if he had any better remembrance of certain facts—of course not giving any inexplicable reason for asking. The result of this inquiry was triumphantly to vindicate the existence of Smith's field as a place near their home, where they used to play in Barking, Essex; and the killing of a cat by another brother was also recollected; while of the swimming of the creek, near a mill-race, full details were given, Frank and Jerry being the heroes of that foolhardy episode."

Sir Oliver Lodge himself appears to believe that he was actually in communication, through Mrs. Piper, with his dead Uncle Jerry; and by spiritists generally this is alluded to as a characteristic instance impossible of explanation on the theory of telepathy between living minds. But it is pertinent to point out that possibly, in his childhood, Sir Oliver may have heard his uncles, in some moment of reminiscence, discussing these very incidents. He would naturally have forgotten the episode, so far as conscious recollection of it was concerned; but he would none the less have retained some memory of their conversation in his subconsciousness, whence Mrs. Piper could have gained knowledge of it telepathically. And, even had he never heard of the incidents, they might indeed have been transmitted to him telepathically from the surviving uncles, and been by him retransmitted to Mrs. Piper.

This last possibility, involving as it does telepathy between more than two persons, may seem to be far-fetched. But there is plenty of evidence that telepathy of this sort—known technically as *telepathie à trois*—is an actuality. I have in mind one particularly interesting case studied by Mr. Andrew Lang, the brilliant essayist and psychical researcher. It concerns a crystal-gazer named Miss Angus.

"Again and again," to give Mr. Lang's own words, "Miss Angus, sitting with man or woman, described acquaintances of theirs but not of hers, in situations not known to the sitters but proved to be true to fact. In one instance, Miss Angus described doings, from three weeks to a fortnight old, of people in India, people whom she had never seen or heard of, but who were known to her sitter. Her account, given on a Saturday, was corroborated by a letter from India, which arrived next day, Sunday. In another case she described—about ten P. M.—what a lady, not known to her, but the daughter of a matron present, who was not the sitter, had been doing about four P. M. on the same day. Again, sitting with a lady, Miss Angus described a singular set of scenes much in the mind, not of her sitter, but of a very unsympathetic stranger, who was reading a book at the other end of the room.

"I have tried every hypothesis, normal and not so normal, to account for these and analogous performances of Miss Angus. There was, in the Indian and other cases, no physical possibility of collusion; chance coincidence did not seem adequate; ghosts were out of the question, so was direct clairvoyance. Nothing remained for the speculative theorizer but the idea of cross currents of telepathy between Miss Angus, a casual stranger, the sitters, and people far away, known to the sitters or the stranger, but unknown to Miss Angus.

"Now," adds Mr. Lang, in a paragraph that every attendant at spiritistic séances would do well to learn by heart, "suppose that Miss Angus, instead of dealing with living people by way of crystal-visions, had dealt by way of voice or automatic handwriting, and had introduced a dead 'communicator.' Then she would have been on a par with Mrs. Piper, yet with no aid from the dead."

That automatists "read the mind" of their sitters, or draw upon the contents of their own subconsciousness in obtaining the facts which they give out as coming from the spirit world, is further evident from experiments in automatic writing conducted by several American and English psychical researchers.[24]

But when they are genuine automatists, it would be unjust to accuse them of conscious deception in attributing their communications to discarnate spirits. The trance state into which they usually fall is an abnormal condition, and is not

[24] The extent to which automatists sometimes draw on the contents of their own subconsciousness is strikingly illustrated by a case investigated by Mr. Lowes Dickinson, wherein the medium, an estimable young lady of his acquaintance, was seemingly "controlled" by the "spirit" of a noblewoman of the Middle Ages, who described the customs, manners, and personages of the country in which she claimed to have lived, in such minute detail and with such accuracy that it seemed certain this was one case at all events in which survival had been proved. Ultimately it was discovered that every fact given by the alleged spirit was contained in a little known historical novel which the medium had read, but read only once, when a very small girl. So far as conscious recollection went she had forgotten all about this book, but subconsciously she had evidently retained a marvelously exact memory of it.

unlike, if not identical with, the hypnotic state. As will be shown in detail later, one of the distinctive characteristics of hypnosis is the preternaturally increased suggestibility of the person hypnotized. He will accept and act upon the slightest suggestion of the hypnotist, no matter how ridiculous and absurd the suggestion may be, so long as it is not repugnant to his moral sense. Moreover, he can be induced to think that he is some one other than his real self, and will often assume the traits of the suggested personality with a fidelity that is astounding.

So, likewise, we must believe, with the automatist, who will impersonate anybody suggested—albeit suggested quite unconsciously—by the sitters, whether it be the "spirit" of a Greek philosopher, an Indian chief, or the deceased friend of some one present. Usually he is so deeply entranced as to have no knowledge of what he is doing, just as the hypnotized subject remains in ignorance of the actions he carries out in response to the operator's suggestions. But there is a record of at least one instance in which the automatist, an amateur psychical researcher named Charles H. Tout, of Vancouver, clearly recognized that his various impersonations were suggested to him by the spectators.

Mr. Tout relates that after attending a few séances with some friends he felt an impulse to play medium himself and assume an alien personality. Yielding to this impulse, he discovered that, without losing complete control of his consciousness, he could develop a secondary self that would impose on the beholders as a discarnate spirit. On one occasion he thus impersonated the "spirit" of a dead woman, the mother of a friend present, and his impersonation was accepted as a genuine case of spirit control. On another, after having given several successful impersonations, he suddenly felt weak and ill. At this point, he states:

"One of the sitters made the remark, which I remember to have overheard, 'It is father controlling him,' and I then seemed to realize who I was and whom I was seeking. I began to be distressed in my lungs, and should have fallen if they had not held me by the hands and let me back gently upon the floor. I was in a measure still conscious of my actions, though not of my surroundings, and I have a clear memory of seeing myself in the character of my dying father lying in the bed and in the room in which he died. It was a most curious sensation. I saw his shrunken hands and face, and lived again through his dying moments; only now I was both myself—in some indistinct sort of way—and my father, with his feelings and appearance."

All of which Mr. Tout rightly attributes to "the dramatic working out, by some half-conscious stratum of his personality, of suggestions made at the time by other members of the circle, or received in prior experiences of the kind."

Add to this the known facts of telepathic action, and there is no need of looking further for a comprehensive explanation of the otherwise perplexing and supernatural-seeming phenomena of psychic automatism. This applies even to the phenomenon of so-called "cross-correspondence," which has been especially stressed the past few years by certain members of the Society for Psychical Research as affording proof positive of survival.

With reference to this particular problem, it should in the first place be said that, in addition to Mrs. Piper, there are a number of other automatic writers who have been similarly investigated by the Society for Psychical Research for a long term of years, and whose trustworthiness has likewise been definitely established. They include a Mrs. Holland, a Mrs. Forbes, a Mrs. Thompson, Mrs. Verrall, of Newnham College, Cambridge, England, and Mrs. Verrall's daughter, Miss Helen Verrall. Through these ladies thousands of alleged "spirit messages" have been received, including many purporting to come from Edmund Gurney, Henry Sidgwick, Frederic Myers, and Richard Hodgson, who in their lifetime were the most active and prominent members of the Society for Psychical Research. And among the automatic writings supposed to emanate from them there have been not a few so peculiarly conditioned as to suggest not only that the "spirits" of the four great psychical researchers are in touch with their living friends, but that they are working hard to devise special tests to prove their identity.

To put the matter more concretely, let me cite the case of Mrs. Holland. This lady is a resident of India. In 1893, having seen in the *Review of Reviews* a reference to automatic writing, she experimented in it herself, and found that she possessed the faculty of penning coherent sentences without being conscious of what she was writing. She continued these experiments for ten years, or until 1903, when, after reading Myers's "Human Personality and its Survival of Bodily Death," she one day discovered that her automatic writing was seemingly no longer spontaneous, but controlled by two outside intelligences that called themselves "Myers" and "Gurney." Each "control," alternating with the other, caused her to write long communications, in which there was mingled with much that seemed unintelligible and nonsensical long descriptions of unnamed persons and places. Her interest aroused, Mrs. Holland collected a number of these communications and mailed them to Miss Alice Johnson, Research Officer of the English Society for Psychical Research.

Examining them carefully, Miss Johnson discovered, much to her surprise, that they contained unmistakable references to people and the homes of people whom Myers and Gurney had known intimately, but of whom, as Miss Johnson satisfied herself by searching inquiry, Mrs. Holland had no knowledge. Thus there was an excellent description of Mrs. Verrall, her husband, Dr. A. W. Verrall, and the Verrall dining-room, in which Myers had often been entertained. Even the street address of the Verralls was correctly given. Miss Johnson, as may be imagined, at once wrote, urging Mrs. Holland to continue her automatic writing, and to forward all her script to the offices of the Society. This was done, with the result that much else of a seemingly evidential value was soon obtained. It was especially noted that, although Mrs. Holland knew nothing of Latin and Greek, her communications from the Myers control occasionally contained passages written in both these languages, with which Myers had been well acquainted.

November 25, 1903, the Gurney control wrote in the automatic script: "Now there is an experiment I want you to make—Suggest to the P. R.—to Miss J.—that some one with a trained will—she will have no difficulty in finding some one of the sort—is to try—for a few minutes—every morning for at least a month—to convey a thought—a phrase—a name—anything they like—to your mind." In due course this suggestion was sent by Mrs. Holland to Miss Johnson, who arranged for a series of such experiments, with Mrs. Verrall acting as the second medium.

The experiments began in March, 1905, were continued until towards the end of May, and were resumed for a few weeks in the spring of the following year. The scheme adopted, however, was not exactly that suggested by the Gurney control. Instead of simply attempting to convey some thought to Mrs. Holland's mind, Mrs. Verrall, at Miss Johnson's suggestion, wrote automatically herself on each day that Mrs. Holland was to write. Neither medium was to hold the slightest communication with the other, but both were to forward their automatic scripts to Miss Johnson as soon as written. In fact, in order to prevent any loophole for fraud, Miss Johnson throughout the 1905 experiments kept Mrs. Holland in ignorance of the identity of her fellow-experimenter, who, on her side, was ignorant of Mrs. Holland's real name—the "Holland" being a pseudonym. Some exceedingly interesting results were secured.

March 1, 1905, Mrs. Holland's script contained these sentences, "There are cut flowers in the blue jar—jonquils I think and tulips—growing tulips near the window. A dull day, but the sky hints at spring, and one chirping bird is heard above the roar of the traffic." In reply to a questioning letter from Miss Johnson, Mrs. Verrall wrote:

"On March 1 the only cut flowers in my drawing-room were in two blue china jars on the mantelpiece; the flowers were large single daffodils. On the ledge of the window ... were three pots of growing yellow tulips—the only flowers near any window. The day was dull in the morning, but about twelve the sun came out and it was warm; it rained heavily in the afternoon."

There was no "cross-correspondence" in the writings of the two scripts for this or the next two weeks—the experimenters wrote only once a week—but in the scripts of the week following Miss Johnson found a curious coincidence—the presence of notes of music. Only once before or since, she testifies, have notes of music appeared in the script of either Mrs. Verrall or Mrs. Holland. In Mrs. Holland's script of that same date, March 22, there was also a reference to "the ivory gate through which all good dreams come." Mrs. Verrall, it was learned, on March 19 or 20, had been reading Virgil's passage in the "Æneid" about the gates of horn and ivory. She had been reading Dante, too, in the original Italian, the first time she had read anything in Italian for months; and, oddly enough, Mrs. Holland's script for March 22 contained a sentence in Italian.

Later scripts were characterized by even more striking correspondences, and—which is not without interest—on more than one occasion the "controls" issued warnings against placing faith in Eusapia Paladino. For instance, on December 1, 1905, the Myers control wrote through Mrs. Holland: "There may be raps genuine enough of their kind—I concede the raps—poltergeist merely—but the luminous appearances—the sounds of a semi-musical nature—the flower falling upon the table—trickery—trickery." And the Gurney control added: "Her feet are very important—Next time can't Miss J. sit with the sapient feet both touching hers—Let her fix her thoughts on the feet and prevent the least movement of them."

As American investigators have since discovered, Eusapia's feet are indeed important.

These first experiments were followed by others, in which, besides Mrs. Holland and Mrs. Verrall, all four of the other mediums mentioned above took part, and again suggestive cross-correspondences were secured. Besides which, having been induced by the results of the Verrall-Holland experiments to study more closely earlier scripts stored in the Society's archives, Miss Johnson discovered what seemed to be similar cross-correspondences that occurred before any experiments of this kind were undertaken. I can give only one or two illustrations. August 28, 1901, Mrs. Forbes wrote a message purporting to come from her dead son Talbot, to the effect that he had to leave her in order to control another "sensitive," and through her obtain corroboration of Mrs. Forbes's own automatic writing. On the same day Mrs. Verrall wrote in Latin of a fir tree planted in a garden, and the script was signed with a sword and a suspended bugle. The latter was part of the badge of the regiment to which Talbot Forbes had belonged, and Mrs. Forbes had in her garden some fir trees grown from seed sent to her by her son. These facts, according to Miss Johnson, were unknown to Mrs. Verrall.

In another case Mrs. Forbes wrote, on November 26 and 27, 1902, references, absolutely meaningless to herself, to a passage in a book which Mrs. Verrall had been reading on those days; and the references also applied appropriately to an obscure sentence in Mrs. Verrall's own script of November 26.

But undoubtedly the most impressive cross-correspondences were obtained in a series of experiments extending from November, 1906, to June, 1907, and involving concordant automatism between Mrs. Holland, in India, and Mrs. Piper, Mrs. Verrall, and Miss Verrall, in England. A full report on this series is given in the October, 1908, issue of the Society's *Proceedings*. The plan followed was to suggest to the controls of Mrs. Piper—in her case the alleged "spirits" of Myers, Sidgwick, and Hodgson—that they transmit to one or more of the other automatists some test word or message. There were many failures, but there were also many seeming successes.

January 16, 1907, the Myers control promised that it would, as a proof of its identity, cause Mrs. Holland and Mrs. Verrall to sign a piece of automatic writing with a triangle drawn within a circle. A circle with a triangle inside it actually appeared in Mrs. Verrall's script of January 28, while a script from Mrs. Holland exhibited several geometrical figures, including a circle with a triangle outside it. February 6 the same control said that it had just been referring, through Mrs. Verrall, to a "library matter," and investigation showed that half an hour earlier Mrs. Verrall, writing at her home in Cambridge, had begun a script in which the word "library" occurred three times—the only time during the period of the experiments that "library" was mentioned in her automatic writing or in Mrs. Piper's trance statements. The Myers control again, on February 11, announced that it had given "hope, star, and Browning" to Mrs. Verrall, and her script showed that this was correct. February 12 the Hodgson control declared it had been trying to impress the word "arrow" on Mrs. Verrall. Her script for the previous day, when received at the Society's offices in London, proved to be decorated with a drawing of three arrows.

It is the multiplicity of coincidences like these—and I have given only the merest fragment of the evidence in hand—that has recently persuaded many hitherto hesitating psychical researchers, notably Sir Oliver Lodge, that scientific proof of spirit communication has veritably been obtained. For myself, I must frankly say, however, that I cannot accept this view of the case. Fraud, I admit, is out of the question as an explanatory hypothesis. Nor does it seem possible to explain away the evidence on the theory of mere chance, guessing, "lucky hits," etc. But there remains the hypothesis of telepathy between living minds; and, as it seems to me, there is nothing whatever in the evidence presented incompatible with the view that the cross-correspondences in question resulted from direct thought transference between the automatists themselves.

CHAPTER V

POLTERGEISTS AND MEDIUMS

WE have now to consider a very different class of spiritistic manifestations, the so-called "physical phenomena," which are historically among the earliest on record, and at the same time are far more spectacular and sensational than the phenomena produced by the automatic speakers and writers. They include such weird occurrences as the appearance in the séance room of ghostly forms alleged to be spirits "materialized" by the power of the medium; the lifting of the latter from the floor by an invisible force; the touching, pinching, and striking of the sitters by unseen hands, and the movement of small articles of furniture as though alive.

Occasionally, when the medium is particularly gifted, still more striking happenings take place. Thus, at a séance with Eusapia Paladino, attended by such eminent scientists as Professors Lombroso, Bianchi, Tamburini, Vizioli, and Ascensi, men whose veracity is beyond question, it is recorded by Lombroso[25] that:

"We saw a great curtain, which separated our room from an alcove adjoining, and which was more than three feet distant from the medium, suddenly move out toward me, envelop me, and wrap me close. Nor was I able to free myself from it except with great difficulty.

"A dish of flour had been put in the little alcove room, at a distance of more than four and a half feet from the medium, who, in her trance, had thought, or, at any rate, spoken, of sprinkling some of the flour in our faces. When light was made, it was found that the dish was bottom side up, with the flour under it. This was dry, to be sure, but coagulated, like gelatine. This circumstance seems to me doubly irreconcilable—first, with the laws of chemistry, and, second, with the power of movement of the medium, who had not only been bound as to her feet, but had her hands held tight by our hands.

"When the lights had been turned on, and we were all ready to go, a great wardrobe that stood in the alcove room, about six and a half feet away from us, was seen advancing slowly towards us. It seemed like a huge pachyderm that was proceeding in leisurely fashion to attack us."

Other investigators, men of equally high character, report marvels no less amazing. On one occasion, Eusapia Paladino is credited with having created an invisible man, a being which the sitters could distinctly feel, although they could

[25] "After Death—What?" pp. 57-58.

not see it, and which, annoyed by their inquisitive prodding, finally turned on one of them and bit him in the thumb. For this we have the authority of Professors Morselli and Barzini, the latter being the investigator whose thumb was bitten.

Again, two English noblemen, Lords Dunraven and Crawford, affirm that they several times saw another medium, the late D. D. Home, floating through the air; once at a height of more than seventy feet above the ground; and that the same medium, by some "spiritual" agency, was elongated in full view of them, so that they beheld his stature visibly increase, to decrease again to normal height only when he came out of the trance condition.[26]

Unfortunately, the "spirits" that perform these uncanny feats have a strong liking for darkness, a circumstance which has led to wholesale, and repeatedly substantiated, accusations of fraud. In fact, there is no other department of spiritism to which the taint of fraud has so thoroughly attached itself. It is obvious that any clever charlatan, by persuading his sitters that darkness is necessary for the development of occult phenomena, can produce most mystifying effects, and the records of scientific investigations, to say nothing of the records of our police courts, abound in evidence that swindlers have not been slow in availing themselves of this opportunity to prey on the credulous and superstitious. The lengths to which bogus mediums will sometimes go, and the extreme gullibility which renders their operations ridiculously easy and highly profitable, are amusingly illustrated by a story told by Mr. Hereward Carrington, an investigator who has done much to make the public acquainted with the ways of fraudulent "psychics."

One of these, according to Mr. Carrington, had among his patrons an elderly business man, the head of a large concern that manufactured farming implements. After several months of intercourse, during which the medium deftly led him on from marvel to marvel, until at last there was no "phenomenon" too incredible for him to swallow, he was informed that at the next séance he would have the unique experience of conversing with the spirit of a deceased inhabitant of the planet Jupiter.

Sure enough, after the lights had been carefully turned low, he was accosted by a tall, shadowy figure, which announced itself as a spirit from Jupiter, and which, speaking excellent English, proceeded to describe the conditions of life in that far-off sphere. The Jupiterians, it appeared, were a poor, ignorant lot, scarcely removed from barbarism; they were greatly in need of civilization, and any one who should help in civilizing them would be generously rewarded in the future life.

"I should be glad to do all in my power," the business man eagerly volunteered, "but I'm afraid there's nothing I could do."

"Yes, indeed, there is. I understand that you make farm implements and machinery. Well, they haven't as much as a spade on Jupiter. If you would send a few tools there, it would be a great step toward civilizing them."

"But how in the world could I get anything to them?"

[26] A detailed account of Home's performances will be found in my book, "Historic Ghosts and Ghost-Hunters," pp. 143-170.

"That is quite simple," the "spirit" glibly explained. "Just send the things to the medium here, and he will dematerialize them and ship them to Jupiter, where they will be rematerialized."

Instead of seeing in this a daring attempt to fleece him, the victim joyfully acquiesced, and sent a number of spades, plows, harrows, etc., to the medium, who promptly disposed of them, not to the people of Jupiter, but to a dealer in such articles. Other séances followed, the spirit from Jupiter again appearing and describing in picturesque language the beneficent consequences of the welcome presents. This meant more gifts, which steadily increased in number and value, until the confederate who had been playing the part of the dead Jupiterian finally became frightened.

"Look here," he told the medium, "this has got to stop. It was all very well when you were satisfied with plows, and rakes, and little things like that, but now that you have got him giving you horses and harvesters there's bound to be trouble. He's sure to find out in the end, and some fine morning we'll wake up on the inside of a jail."

"Oh, don't worry," said the medium. "He'll never find out anything."

"I'm not so certain of that. At any rate, you'll have to get somebody to take my place."

One word led to another, and ended in a violent quarrel. The confederate, vowing vengeance, called on the business man, and told him how he had been duped. He was met with the astonishing reply:

"I don't believe a word you say."

"You don't?" he cried. "Didn't you send the medium, only yesterday, a horse and cart to be dematerialized?"

"Yes."

"Well, if you wish to know where they are, come with me. He has them in a stable near his house, waiting to find a buyer."

Together they went to the stable, where the confederate pointed out the horse and cart that had been given to the medium. In particular, he identified the cart by the number painted on it.

"Come, now," said he, "you can't deny that's your cart, can you?"

"Why," was the answer, "it does indeed look like my cart. But I know it isn't."

"How do you know it isn't?"

"Because"—in a tone of solemn conviction—"I know that by this time my cart is on Jupiter."

In another case, drawn to my attention by a lawyer friend, the victim was a well-to-do Boston merchant, who had become interested in spiritism shortly after the death of his wife, to whom he had been devotedly attached, and with whose spirit he hoped to be brought into communication. A medium, learning this, determined to profit from his grief and longing, and hired a young woman to pose as the spirit of the dead wife. He was then told that before long it would be possible to "materialize" his wife from the spirit world with such substantiality that he would be able to clasp her in his arms.

When the appointed time came, a slender form, draped in gauze, emerged from the mediumistic cabinet into the darkened séance room, and saluted him with a joyful cry of "Husband!" There was not light enough to see the "spirit's" face, but he did not for an instant doubt that he was really gazing at his wife, and rose to embrace her. At once the figure vanished, and after the lights were turned up the medium explained that there would have to be a good many "materializations" before the spirit form would be solid enough for him to touch it.

This meant, of course, numerous séances, for which the deluded husband paid handsomely. It also helped to blind him to the true state of affairs, and increased his infatuation to such an extent that when at length the "spirit" submitted to his caresses, it did not seem at all incongruous to find that he was pressing to his breast a flesh-and-blood woman.

The medium now resolved on a bold stroke. Acting under her instruction, the "spirit" bitterly complained one evening that she did not possess any jewelry.

"What!" her "husband" exclaimed. "Do you mean to say that they wear jewelry in the other world?"

"Oh, yes. But nothing to compare with what I had while on earth. What have you done with mine?"

"I have it all—every piece—put away in a little box."

"Good. Then if you will bring it to-morrow night, I can take it with me when I leave you. The medium, you know, can dematerialize it for us."

"I will bring it. Rest assured of that."

Alas for husbandly devotion! The séance at which he turned over the jewelry to the affectionate "spirit" of his wife was the last at which he held communion with her. When he next called, he was told that the medium had been unexpectedly summoned out of town. She never came back.

These two episodes are typical rather than exceptional instances of the sort of thing that has been going on for years in connection with the physical phenomena of spiritism. Its continuance has been made possible largely by a widespread belief, entertained not by the ignorant and superstitious merely, but by men of distinction in the intellectual and scientific world, that, notwithstanding the prevalence of fraud, there are at least some physical phenomena which must be accounted genuine.

Men like the Italian savants already named, the English naturalist, Alfred Russel Wallace; the great chemist, Sir William Crookes; the French astronomer, Camille Flammarion, and many others who might be mentioned, are satisfied that they have witnessed in the séance room occurrences out of all accord with natural laws, and not to be attributed to fraud.

In support of this view, emphasis is laid on the fact that, leaving out of consideration all mediums who employ their powers as a means of livelihood, physical phenomena of the most bizarre sort have been manifested through men and women in private life, who cannot possibly have a pecuniary motive for deception, and whose character is beyond reproach.

One of the most celebrated of physical mediums, in fact, was a clergyman of the Church of England, the Reverend W. Stainton Moses, a gentleman respected and warmly esteemed by all who knew him.[27]

As a further argument in behalf of the authenticity of certain of the phenomena, attention is also called to the interesting circumstance that, long before spiritism and spiritistic mediums were heard of, similar marvels—including seemingly spontaneous movements of furniture, and the occurrence of mysterious raps, knockings, and other noises—were frequently reported by thoroughly reputable witnesses.

To mention only a few cases,[28] as long ago as 1661 there was an outbreak of this kind at the home of a wealthy Englishman named Mompesson, an invisible ghost for months disturbing the peace of the Mompesson family by beating on a drum, banging at doors, tugging at bedclothes, and hurling household articles about in a most destructive manner. The affair made so much stir that a royal commission was sent to inquire into it, but signally failed to lay the ghost. For nearly a year, in 1716-1717, the Reverend Samuel Wesley, father of the founder of Methodism, was tormented in like fashion at his rectory in Lincolnshire. In 1753 a Russian monastery was invaded by an equally malicious and equally invisible "spirit," which for months amused itself by ringing the monastery bells at unseemly hours. Nine years later all London was thrilled by the celebrated Cock Lane ghost, which produced spirit rappings with as much éclat as the most up-to-date, medium-invoked visitant from "the other side." In none of these instances did contemporary investigators find a wholly satisfactory explanation for the singular phenomena involved.

Nevertheless, it may confidently be affirmed that, instead of strengthening the case for the physical phenomena of spiritism, the doings of the poltergeists—as these tricky ghosts are called by psychical researchers—considerably weaken it. For during recent years a number of poltergeist hauntings have been looked into by members of the Society for Psychical Research, and whenever the conditions have been such as to permit a thorough investigation, it has been found that, so far from being spiritual entities, poltergeists are invariably compounded of deceit, credulity, and delusion. Even more important, from the standpoint of getting at the true inwardness of physical mediumship, the discovery has been made that fraud has frequently been practised in poltergeist cases without any apparent motive.

Again I will give an instance from actual occurrence, in order to make my meaning perfectly clear. Word was one day received at the London offices of the

---

[27] An excellent study of the mediumship of Stainton Moses is contained in Frank Podmore's "Modern Spiritualism," vol. ii, pp. 276-288.

[28] Studied in detail in my book, "Historic Ghosts and Ghost-Hunters."

Society for Psychical Research that a ghost had taken possession of a farmhouse in Shropshire, and was making life miserable for the lawful occupants, a family named Hampson and their two maidservants, Priscilla Evans and Emma Davies. Nobody saw the ghost, but it made its presence felt in true poltergeist style.

It had announced its advent, about four o'clock one fine afternoon, by lifting a saucepan from the kitchen fire and throwing it across the room, picking red-hot coals out of the fire and scattering them over the floor, and by causing a lamp globe to fly miraculously through the air. This last prank, naturally enough, so frightened the Hampsons and their servants that they fled from the house, and summoned aid from the nearest neighbors, among them a Mr. Lea, who, in the report that reached the Society for Psychical Research,[29] declared that when he approached the Hampson homestead, it seemed as if all the upstairs rooms were on fire, "as there was such a light in the windows."

Reënforced, the Hampsons made bold to enter the house again, but the poltergeist had seemingly formed a strong dislike to them, for the report added:

"As things were continuing to jump about the kitchen in a manner which was altogether inexplicable, and many were getting damaged, Hampson decided to remove everything out of the apartment. He accordingly took down a barometer from the wall, when something struck him on the leg, and a loaf of bread, which was on the table, was thrown by some invisible means, and hit him on the back. A volume of 'Pilgrim's Progress' was thrown, or jumped, through the window, and a large, ornamental sea-shell went through in similar fashion.

"In the parlor a sewing machine was thrown about and damaged. The nurse girl was nursing the baby by the fire when some fire leaped from the grate, and the child's hair was singed and its arms burned. The girl was so alarmed that she set off to a neighbor's, and on the way there her clothes took fire, and had to be torn from her body. During the evening, while the girl was at the neighbor's, a plate, which she touched while having her supper, was repeatedly thrown on the floor, and the pieces were picked up by some unseen agency, and put in the center of the table."

On the girl's return to the Hampson place the manifestations broke out anew. Mr. and Mrs. Lea were strongly of the opinion that they were the work of the devil; the Hampsons, however, inclined to the view that the blame lay at the door of some evil spirit that was especially desirous of tormenting the nurse girl, Emma Davies, it being noticed that things quieted down whenever she was out of the house. On this theory they sent her to her home in a neighboring village, where the poltergeist continued to annoy her. In the presence of a police officer, watching her closely to detect evidence of fraud, it wrenched the buttons from her dress and ripped out the stitches of her apron. While the village schoolmistress and some twenty other people looked on, it twice drew off her shoes and tossed them to the opposite side of the room; and it was said to have afterward lifted her bodily from the floor, and held her suspended in mid-air.

Clearly, this was a case calling for investigation, and the Society for Psychical

[29] Proceedings of the Society for Psychical Research, vol. xii, pp. 58-67.

Research at once commissioned one of its expert detectives of the supernatural, Mr. F. S. Hughes, to proceed to the scene of the disturbances. But before he arrived, the mystery was solved. The girl, it seems, had been made so nervous and excited by the unwelcome attentions of the poltergeist that it was thought best to place her in a physician's care, and she was accordingly taken to a sanitarium and kept in strict seclusion, under the constant observation of the physician's housekeeper, Miss Turner, a shrewd, level-headed woman. For three days, the poltergeist continued to plague her. Then it suddenly took its departure, under the following circumstances, narrated by Mr. Hughes in his official report:

"On Tuesday morning Miss Turner was in an upper room at the back of the house, and the servant of the establishment and Emma Davies were outside, Emma having her back to the house, and unaware that she was observed. Miss Turner noticed that she had a piece of brick in her hand, held behind her back. This she threw to a distance by a turn of the wrist, and, while doing so, screamed to attract the attention of the servant, who, of course, turning round, saw the brick in the air, and was very much frightened. Emma Davies, looking round, saw that she had been seen by Miss Turner, and, apparently imagining that she had been found out, was very anxious to return home that night.

"Miss Turner took no notice of the occurrence at the time, but the next morning she asked the girl if she had been playing tricks, and the girl confessed that she had, and went through some of the performances very skillfully, according to Miss Turner's account. Later on in the day she repeated these in the presence of the doctor, Miss Turner, and two reporters from London."

Obviously, trickster though she was, the girl had no rational motive for her conduct. It had already cost her a good position, and rendered it most unlikely that she would easily get another. And, in fact, this same absence of motive is conspicuous in nearly all the poltergeist cases exposed by the Society for Psychical Research, and by independent investigators. It is also noteworthy that when discovery is made, the active agent is usually found to be a boy or girl, man or woman, constitutionally or temporarily in an abnormal nervous condition.

In this particular case, for instance, the girl, Emma Davies, on the testimony of her mother, was subject to "fits." In another case, investigated by the Society, the poltergeist was definitely identified with a little deformed girl, twelve years old, of decidedly abnormal characteristics. In a third case, investigated by Mr. Frank Podmore, another member of the Society and a specialist on poltergeists, a confession of fraud was elicited from a neurotic boy of fifteen—a confession only partial, it is true, but in one sense more illuminating than any full confession would have been. The case is so instructive, both for its revelation of the almost incredible credulity of many devotees of spiritism, and for the light it throws on the problems of physical mediumship, that I quote it, condensed, from Mr. Podmore's detailed review of his investigation.[30]

"In the autumn of 1894," he states, "Mrs. B., a lady living in a provincial town, gave me an account of certain curious incidents which had recently taken place

[30] Proceedings of the Society for Psychical Research, vol. xii, pp. 101-103.

in her house. The occupants of the house—an old one—consisted, besides Mrs. B. and her family, of a widow lady, Mrs. D., and her two children, a girl of about twenty, C. D., and a boy of fifteen, E. D.

"Mrs. B., C. D., and E. D. had been in the habit of trying experiments with planchette in the evening. Planchette had given them to understand that the house was haunted by four spirits, a wicked marquis, a wicked monk, a lay desperado, and a virtuous and beautiful young lady. These spirits wrote, through planchette, of treasure concealed in the house, of a hidden chamber, and many other matters. Among other proofs were the following:

"One evening after dark, Mrs. B., in accordance with directions received through planchette, went with C. D. and E. D. to an old oak tree in the garden, and, standing with the girl and boy on either side, holding a hand of each, she distinctly heard a stone strike the garden roller a few feet off. The phenomenon was repeated twice; and her companions solemnly assured her that they had no part in the performance.

"On another occasion, sitting in a bedroom in the dark, with only E. D. in the room, Mrs. B. was struck by a stone on the temple, heard objects thrown about the room, felt an arm put through hers, and so on. Some of these phenomena occurred when she was alone in the room—but with the door, I gathered, not shut.

"Mrs. B. one morning placed a white chrysanthemum bouquet on the boughs of the oak tree. It disappeared shortly afterward, and on the next morning two other small bouquets were found there. Mrs. B. asked for whom these were intended, and went away, leaving pencil and paper. On her return she found the paper torn in half, and the initials of her own Christian name, and that of C. D., written on the two halves respectively, with a bouquet on each half.

"About this time a secret chamber was discovered with the skeleton of a cat crouching in act to spring, and the skeleton of a woman. Asked more particularly about the latter, Mrs. B. said: 'Well, at least a skull and some bones—but it was a woman's skull.'

"A few days after receiving this account, I went down by invitation to the house. I saw Mrs. D. and her two children, and received from them ungrudging corroboration of Mrs. B.'s marvelous story. In E. D.'s company I penetrated the secret chamber, and found there the mummified skeleton of what might have been a cat—but nothing else. In removing the stains left by this exploit, I contrived a tête-à-tête interview with E. D., and asked him: 'How much did you do of all these things?' He replied: 'Oh, not much. I only did a few little things.'

"Pressed on particular points, he admitted having thrown *one* stone at the garden roller, and having also thrown a trouser button against the wall when sitting alone in the bedroom with Mrs. B. He denied having produced the other phenomena on those occasions. Asked as to the bouquets, he said he had not placed them on the tree. Pressed a little more, he said: 'If I did it, it must have been without knowing it.' This without any suggestion from me as to possible somnambulism, or unconscious action. He assured me that his sister had had no hand in this matter. I could not get any more out of him, as he was shortly after called away.

"I subsequently learned from his mother that E. D. was so nervous and delicate that he slept in her room at night; that he was not allowed to do much mental work; that he was subject to attacks of somnambulism; and had, indeed, fallen into a semiconscious state only a few days before, during a lesson in carpentry."

Probably the whole affair originated in a moment of mischief, and was carried on and elaborated because of an uncontrollable, and perhaps not entirely conscious, desire on the part of the abnormally conditioned lad to mystify the too easily imposed upon elderly lady.

In point of fact, the investigations of the Society for Psychical Research make it certain that in nine cases out of ten a poltergeist is a by-product of hysteria, using the term in its strictest medical sense. As is well known, one of the distinctive symptoms of hysteria is a tendency to indulge in all manner of lies and deceptions, coupled often with almost diabolical cleverness in giving these lies and deceptions a color of reality. Impulse to such trickery may arise from a great variety of motives; frequently, it would seem, from nothing more than an abnormal craving for notoriety and admiration. Certainly, the hysterical young people run to earth by the poltergeist hunters of the Society for Psychical Research did not engage in their hoaxings because they expected to make money out of them.

The bearing of all this on the physical phenomena of spiritism is surely self-evident. It shows, for one thing, that the money motive is not the only motive inciting mediums to fraud; that when a neurotic or hysterical condition is present, the best of characters is no guarantee against duplicity; and that under such circumstances the detection of fraud is exceedingly difficult, particularly in the case of witnesses predisposed to regard the phenomena as genuine. If hysterical children can, as they have often done, carry on a course of deception mystifying a whole community, it is manifest that mediums of similar hysterical tendencies, working under cover of darkness or in a dim light, can more or less readily deceive the most expert observers; and, moreover, that they may be only partially, if at all, conscious of their own frauds.[31]

Further, in estimating the nature of the phenomena produced at the séances of physical mediums, it is imperative to take into account the innumerable possibilities of mal-observation on the part of the spectators. Experience has shown that comparatively few people, no matter how honest, are trustworthy witnesses even when conditions for observation are of the best.

For proof of this, one does not need to look beyond the courtroom, where every day perfectly honest people give the most contradictory accounts of some simple occurrence. If it is thus difficult to see correctly what goes on in the broad light of day, it surely is far more difficult to be certain of exactly what is happening in a room where there is darkness rather than light. Besides which, the imaginative faculty may be excited to such an extent that the sitters at a séance may not only be misled into making inaccurate reports of what really occurred, but they may even, and with absolute sincerity, testify to phenomena which did not occur at all.

[31] I am inclined, for example, to believe that there is a large element of hysteria in the mediumship of the discredited Eusapia Paladino, once the marvel of two continents.

A friend of mine, now a physician in Maryland, used to amuse himself in his student days by playing medium at table-tipping séances. He would cause the table to rap out messages to various acquaintances of his, none of whom were spiritists, but several of whom became intensely interested, owing to their inability to fathom the source of the communications they received, my friend managing things so skillfully that they did not suspect him of hoaxing them.

One evening the table announced the presence of the "spirit" of a little child, the daughter of a lady well known to most of the sitters. They were not aware, however, that my friend was intimately acquainted with the little one's life history, and when, utilizing this knowledge, he proceeded to make the table rap communications of a most personal character, there was considerable excitement. Suddenly a lady present, not a relative of the dead child, uttered a piercing scream, and fainted.

When she was revived, she declared, with emphatic assurance, that she had seen the head of a child emerge from the center of the table.

Equally indicative of the part imagination plays in constructing spiritistic phenomena is an experience of my own with a New York medium. His specialty was materialization, but at the séance in question he did not attempt to develop "spirit forms" by any of the methods in vogue among materializers. Instead, the gas having been lowered until the room was almost in total darkness, he went into a "trance," and, seated at the séance table, with his head resting on his hands, declaimed in a singsong voice:

"The spirits are coming. I can feel them approaching. You will be able to see them soon. They are almost here. Here is one now, on my left. Can't you see it? And here comes another, and another. They are crowding around me, so anxious to communicate with you. Can't you see them? I can't hold them long; they will be gone soon. Oh, can't you see them?"

There were, perhaps, a dozen people present, including myself and a fellow investigator, who had accompanied me. Of the others, three responded to the hypnotic suggestiveness of the medium's words and manner, and solemnly declared that they could see a "spirit" hovering about him. One lady, whose integrity I could not doubt, insisted that she saw two "spirits," which she identified as her dead husband and brother.

Undoubtedly, therefore, it is proper to assume that when, in the instances cited at the beginning of this chapter, Professor Lombroso, sitting with Eusapia Paladino, saw a huge wardrobe advance to attack him; and when Lords Crawford and Dunraven saw the medium Home floating through the air, hallucination rather than "spirit action" is the correct explanation. At all events, in view of the known fallibility of the human senses; the manifold opportunities for fraud open to mediums; and the fact that, with the single exception of Home, every medium subjected to scientific investigation has been caught practising fraud at one time or another, it seems extremely rash to accept as genuine any of the phenomena of physical mediumship.

Still, it would be incorrect to say that the time devoted by psychical researchers to the investigation of these phenomena has been time wasted. They have performed a necessary police duty for society, and their labors, as we shall see, have been productive of psychological discoveries of great practical importance.

CHAPTER VI

THE SUBCONSCIOUS

WHEN the Society for Psychical Research was founded, in 1882, its purpose was not only to obtain, if possible, scientifically acceptable proof of the survival of human personality after bodily death, but also to study the nature of personality in its mundane aspects, with a view to securing greater insight into the powers and possibilities of man here on earth.

In this latter quest it has been eminently successful, and thanks to its labors our knowledge of ourselves has been increased a thousandfold. As has been shown, phenomena hitherto regarded as mysterious and "supernatural"—such as apparitions, clairvoyance, crystal-gazing, etc.—have been definitely explained on a purely naturalistic basis; and, as was said at the close of the last chapter, in addition to naturalizing the supernatural, psychical researchers have made, or have assisted in making, discoveries of great practical utility, and having a profound bearing on affairs of everyday life.

Among these, none is of more importance than the discovery of the "subconscious." This term, which was almost unheard of a few years ago, is nowadays used by psychologists in a variety of ways, but it may be broadly defined as including an extensive range of mental processes and phenomena that occur beneath the surface of our ordinary consciousness. Subconscious mental action, in fact, has a constant, unceasing part in our lives. It is in evidence in such commonplace acts as walking, talking, writing, playing the piano, handling a tool, a tennis racket, or a baseball bat.

There was a time, in the experience of all of us, when we could do none of these things, but had to learn them by conscious effort. Little by little, as we acquired more skill, the element of consciousness became less and less, until at last we could execute them in a seemingly automatic manner, as in the fashion of the piano player described by Miss Cobbe:

"Two different lines of hieroglyphics have to be read at once, and the right hand has to be guided to attend to one of them, the left to the other. All the fingers have the work assigned as quickly as they can move. The mind, or something which does duty as mind, interprets scores of A sharps, and B flats, and C naturals into black ivory keys and white ones, crotchets, and quavers, and demi-quavers, rests, and all the mysteries of music. The feet are not idle, but have something to do with the pedals. And all this time the performer, the *conscious* performer, is in a seventh heaven of artistic rapture at the results of all this tremendous business, or perchance lost in a flirtation with the individual who turns the leaves of the music book, and is justly persuaded she is giving him the whole of her soul."

The subconscious is thus a sort of reservoir in which are stored up, available for future use, the things learned through education and experience; and it also has a dynamic power that enables it to supplement, economize, and enlarge the operations of the upper consciousness. Ordinarily we fail to appreciate what we owe to this hidden servitor, for the reason that its workings are so smooth, so unobtrusive, as to pass quite unnoticed. Yet abundant evidence has been secured to demonstrate not simply the fact of its existence, but the more significant fact that it is never at rest, but is perpetually laboring in our behalf.

Even when our consciousness is for the moment completely in abeyance—as when we are asleep—the subconscious continues operant. Many of my readers have doubtless had the experience of vainly endeavoring for hours, perhaps for days, to solve some important problem, and then awaking one morning with a luminously clear idea of its correct solution. While they slept, their subconsciousness had been at work disentangling the threads of their conscious reasoning, stripping away and discarding unessentials, and finally presenting them with, so to speak, a ready-made understanding of that which had previously been so perplexing to them.

In all such cases the action of the subconscious is more vividly evident when, as often happens, the desired solution is gained during sleep itself, in the form of a dream. An excellent example is found in an episode narrated by a business man, who says:

"I had been bothered since September with an error in my cash account for that month, and, despite many hours' examination, it defied all my efforts, and I almost gave it up as hopeless. It had been the subject of my waking thoughts for many nights, and had occupied a large portion of my leisure hours. Matters remained thus unsettled until the eleventh of December. On this night I had not, to my knowledge, once thought of the subject, but I had not been long in bed and asleep, when my brain was as busy with the books as though I had been at my desk.

"The cash book, banker's pass books, etc., etc., appeared before me; and, without any apparent trouble, I almost immediately discovered the cause of the mistakes, which had arisen out of a complicated cross entry. I perfectly recollect having taken a slip of paper in my dream, and made such a memorandum as would enable me to correct the error at some leisure time; and, having done this, that the whole of the circumstances had passed from my mind.

"When I awoke in the morning I had not the slightest recollection of my dream, nor did it once occur to me throughout the day, although I had the very books before me on which I had apparently been engaged in my sleep. When I returned home in the afternoon, as I did early, for the purpose of dressing, and proceeded to shave, I took up a piece of paper from my dressing table to wipe my razor, and you may imagine my surprise at finding thereon the very memorandum I fancied

I had made during the previous night. The effect on me was such that I returned to our office and turned to the cash book, when I found that I had really, while asleep, detected the error which I could not detect in my waking hours, and had actually jotted it down at the time.

"I have no recollection whatever as to where I obtained the paper and pencil with which I made the memorandum. It certainly must have been written in the dark, and in my bedroom, as I found both paper and pencil there the following afternoon. The pencil was not one which I am in the habit of carrying, and my impression is that I must either have found it in the room, or gone down-stairs for it."[32]

Illustrative of the same subconscious mechanism, and doubly interesting because of the light it throws on the true nature of many dreams frequently regarded as supernatural, is a singular experience that once befell Professor H. V. Hilprecht, the well-known archæologist of the University of Pennsylvania.

At the time, Professor Hilprecht was trying to decipher the inscriptions on two small fragments of agate from the temple of Bel in ancient Babylonia, and believed by him to be portions of the finger rings of some wealthy Babylonian. He had already published a preliminary report on the collection of which they formed a part, but, despite weeks of earnest effort, had utterly failed to get at the meaning of the words inscribed on them.

One Saturday night, after working on the fragments until nearly twelve o'clock without any satisfactory result, he went to bed weary and exhausted, and was soon in a deep sleep. He then dreamed that he was transported to the temple of Bel, where a venerable priest, whose dress showed that he belonged to a pre-Christian epoch, conducted him into the treasure chamber of the temple. It was a small, low room, without windows, and contained a large wooden chest, around which were scattered pieces of agate and other valuable stones. While Professor Hilprecht stood looking at these, the priest said to him:

"The two fragments which you have published separately upon pages 22 and 26 belong together, are not finger rings, and their history is as follows:

"King Kurigalzu [who reigned in Babylonia about 1300 B. C.], once sent to the temple of Bel, among other articles of agate and lapis lazuli, an inscribed votive cylinder of agate. Then we priests suddenly received the command to make for the statue of the god Ninib a pair of earrings of agate. We were in great dismay, since there was no agate at hand as raw material. In order to execute the command, there was nothing for us to do but cut the votive cylinder into three parts, making three rings, each of which contained a portion of the original inscription.

"The first two rings served as earrings for the statue of the god; the two fragments which have given you so much trouble are portions of them. If you will put the two together you will have confirmation of my words. But the third ring you have not yet found in the course of your excavations, and you never will find it."

With this the priest disappeared, and the dream came to an end. In the morn-

[32] Proceedings of the Society for Psychical Research, vol. viii, pp. 394-395.

ing, impressed with its coherence and vividness, Professor Hilprecht again attacked the troublesome fragments, put them together as directed, and, by making the proper guesses for the missing middle portion, readily deciphered the full inscription: "To the god Ninib, son of Bel, his lord, has Kurigalzu, pontifex of Bel, presented this."[33]

Nor are the intellectual achievements of the subconscious during sleep confined to the solution of problems that have been vexing the upper consciousness. It has a highly original, creative power of its own. Thus the composer Tartini dreamed one night that he heard the devil playing a wonderful sonata, and, remembering it on awaking, was able to set it down on paper, and thereby put to his credit one of the finest pieces of music that bears his name. Coleridge's "Kubla Khan" was another dream composition; and, indeed, a long list of masterpieces in music, art, and literature, originating through subconscious mental action in sleep, might be drawn up.

A typical case was recently communicated to me by a well-known Pacific Coast architect, Mr. B. J. S. Cahill. He had been commissioned to design a twenty-six-story office building, to be erected in Portland, Oregon, and he determined, if possible, to plan one that would be a real contribution towards the solution of some of the most difficult problems of modern commercial architecture. For weeks Mr. Cahill labored hard to devise a building that would unite a maximum of beauty, solidity, and capacity with an abundance, and as nearly as possible an equality, of light and air for the many offices it was to contain. The structure he ultimately conceived was certainly novel, and differed conspicuously from the ordinary four-sided office building, with its inner offices lighted from a court.

His plan called for the construction of a building shaped much like a St. Andrew's cross, or like a square with a triangle cut out of each side. In this way the need for an inner court was completely obviated, and the only poorly ventilated and dimly lighted portion of the building would be its central "core." Here the elevators and stairs were to be located.

According to the architect's own statement, this plan—which has been highly praised by so eminent a critic as Mr. Montgomery Schuyler—was born in his mind while he slept. One night he saw in a dream a building shaped in this fashion, and knew that his problem was solved. He tells me that on awaking he made two rough sketches of the plan in a pocket note-book—one showing the general design, the other indicating the appearance of the building when completed.

Perhaps no one has ever been more favored in this same way than that remarkable man of genius, the late Robert Louis Stevenson. The plots for many of Stevenson's best stories—including the marvelous "Doctor Jekyll and Mr. Hyde"—came to him in dreams, as he himself has related in a delightful autobiographical essay, in which, with characteristic whimsicality, he personifies his subconscious ideas as "Brownies" and "little people."

"This dreamer, like many other persons," he says, "has encountered some trifling vicissitudes of fortune. When the bank begins to send letters, and the butcher

[33] Proceedings of the Society for Psychical Research, vol. xii, pp. 14-15.

to linger at the back gates, he sets to belaboring his brains after a story, for that is his readiest money winner; and behold! at once the little people begin to bestir themselves in the same quest, and labor all night long, and all night long set before him truncheons of tales upon their lighted theater. No fear of his being frightened now; the flying heart and the frozen scalp are things bygone; applause, growing applause, growing interest, growing exultation in his own cleverness—for he takes all the credit—and at last a jubilant leap to wakefulness, with the cry: 'I have it, that'll do!' upon his lips; with such and similar emotions he sits at these nocturnal dreams, with such outbreaks, like Claudius in the play, he scatters the performance in the midst.

"Often enough the waking is a disappointment; he has been too deep asleep, as I explain the thing; drowsiness has gained his little people; they have gone stumbling and maundering through their parts; and the play, to the wakened mind, is seen to be a tissue of absurdities. And yet how often have these sleepless Brownies done him honest service, and given him, as he sat idly taking his pleasure in the boxes, better tales than he could fashion for himself.

"The more I think of it," Stevenson continues, "the more I am moved to press upon the world my question: 'Who are the little people?' They are near connections of the dreamer's, beyond doubt; they share in his financial worries, and have an eye to the bank book; they share plainly in his training; they have plainly learned, like him, to build the scheme of a considerable story, and to arrange emotion in progressive order; only I think they have more talent; and one thing is beyond doubt—they can tell him a story piece by piece, like a serial, and keep him all the while in ignorance of where they aim.

"That part of my work which is done while I am sleeping is the Brownies' part beyond contention; but that which is done when I am up and about is by no means necessarily mine, since all goes to show the Brownies have a hand in it even then."[34]

It is worth noting that facts like these have recently led to a novel theory explanatory of what is known as "genius." Instead of adopting the Lombrosian doctrine, and regarding the man of genius as a kind of transcendental degenerate, this latest theory affirms that he is what he is by reason of enjoying a readier communication than most men possess between the conscious and subconscious portions of his mind. Such a view has the further virtue of being completely in accord with the familiar definition of genius as an infinite capacity for hard work.

From what has been said, it must be evident that the contents of the subconscious are made up in large measure of knowledge gained at one time or another by conscious endeavor and thought. The man who thinks hard consciously, is certain to have a richer fund of subconscious information at his disposal than the one whose conscious thinking is of the idle, futile, scatter-brained sort. All successful men, whether a Milton or a Rockefeller, a Shakespeare or a Morgan, are men who have developed their subconscious faculties by laborious application of their conscious powers in the routine of daily life.

---

[34] Quoted from the "Chapter on Dreams," in R. L. Stevenson's "Across the Plains."

On the other hand, it has also to be observed that knowledge is often obtained subconsciously without passing through any preliminary stage of conscious attention and awareness; and that, by a reversal of the usual process, the conscious frequently acquires from the subconscious information of which it would otherwise be ignorant.

I have previously alluded to this interesting and most important fact in my discussion of telepathy, clairvoyance, crystal-gazing, and kindred problems in psychical research. As we then saw, the subconscious has a certain eerie faculty of imparting its information to the upper consciousness in the way of hallucinations, indicative at times of thought transference from mind to mind, or, more commonly, originating merely from unnoticed impressions of direct, personal experience.

It cannot be too firmly borne in mind that every day of our lives we see and hear and feel more than we realize; that these unobserved sights and sounds and sensations may, nevertheless, be subconsciously registered in our minds; and that they may soon or late be projected above the threshold of consciousness in a form astonishing, puzzling, and perhaps annoying to us, as in the case of a strange experience of a young New York newspaper man.

It was his business to edit for publication in a number of country newspapers the dispatches sent in by a telegraphic news agency. He had been thus engaged for perhaps a year when he noticed, greatly to his dismay, that he was repeatedly omitting items which he believed, on reading them in the telegraphic copy, to be "old news," but which were printed with more or less prominence in the next morning's issues of other newspapers. This occurred so often that he began to tremble for his position, and set himself earnestly to solve the mystery.

Luckily he had some acquaintance with psychology, and knew that his trouble must be due to a faulty identification of subconscious with conscious impressions. But why was it, he asked himself, that on certain nights he would be quite free from such errors of judgment, while on others he might omit, or be strongly tempted to omit, on the ground of supposed previous publication, half a dozen items of real news value? The truth dawned on him one evening as he was sitting down to begin work.

On his desk lay a heap of envelopes containing the dispatches that had come from the news agency before his arrival at the newspaper office. These should already have been opened by an office boy, but that night he had been busy with something else. Mechanically, the editor himself tore open the envelopes, smoothed out their contents, and, without reading them, made a neat pile of the typewritten sheets, preparatory to going through them.

He had not been working an hour when he came to a dispatch, which he tossed aside, with the muttered comment, "That's an old story, sure. I've read it somewhere before."

Then, remembering the mistakes he had been making, he hesitated, picked it up, and read it carefully. Every word in it seemed familiar. But where could he have read it? In the evening papers? He went through them one by one, without result. Then it suddenly occurred to him that possibly, in opening the dispatches, he had, without being aware of it, glanced at this particular item, and had obtained a subconscious knowledge of it, which was now welling up confusedly as a conscious memory.

To test this theory, he directed the office boy to open the dispatches without fail for the next few nights. On none of these did he suffer from memory confusion.

Possibly, if he had analyzed the matter further, he would have found that the news items which had caught his eye while smoothing out the dispatch sheets related to subjects of some special interest to him. For just as one's conscious attention is arrested by that which is particularly interesting, so does the subconscious select for presentation to the upper consciousness information of temporary or habitual interest and significance.

Sometimes, too, there is involved a harking back to interests of an earlier period of life. A simple but instructive illustration of this is found in a little incident that occurred to Doctor Richard Hodgson while on a visit to England. It may best be reported in his own words:[35]

"Yesterday morning (September 13, 1895), just after breakfast, I was strolling alone along one of the garden paths of Leckhampton House, Cambridge, repeating aloud to myself the verses of a poem. I became temporarily oblivious to my garden surroundings, and regained my consciousness of them suddenly, to find myself brought to a stand, in a stooping position, gazing intently at a five-leaved clover. On careful examination, I found about a dozen specimens of five-leaved clover, as well as several specimens of four-leaved clover, all of which probably came from the same root.

"Several years ago I was interested in getting extra-leaved clovers, but I have not for years made any active search for them, though occasionally my conscious attention, as I walked along, has been given to appearances of four-leaved clover, which proved, on examination, to be deceptive. The peculiarity of yesterday's 'find' was that I discovered myself, with a sort of shock, standing still and stooping down, and afterward realized that a five-leaved clover was directly under my eyes."

Compare with this an incident reported by an English clergyman, the Reverend P. H. Newnham. We find in it exactly the same element of selective subconscious attention, accompanied, however, by an auditory hallucination as a means of notifying the upper consciousness of the fact subconsciously observed.

"I was visiting friends at Tunbridge Wells," says Mr. Newnham, "and went out one evening, entomologizing. As I crossed a stile into a field, on my way to a neighboring wood, a voice said distinctly in my right ear: 'You'll find "Chaonia" on that oak.' This was a very scarce moth, which I had never seen before, and which most assuredly I had never consciously thought of seeing. There were several oaks in the field, but I instinctively walked up to one, straight to the off side of it, and there was the moth indicated."[36]

---

[35] Proceedings of the Society for Psychical Research, vol. xi, p. 415.

[36] Proceedings of the Society for Psychical Research, vol. xi, p. 411.

The psychological explanation of this is simple enough, and is equally applicable to similar, if more sensational, hallucinations widely heralded as of supernatural character. It is manifestly absurd to suppose that a "spirit" announced to the entomologizing clergyman the presence of the rare and greatly sought-after moth which it was his good fortune to capture. But it is not at all absurd to suggest that quite likely, although he had consciously forgotten all about it, he had at some time seen Chaonia, or an entomological text-book picture of Chaonia; that he had subconsciously caught a glimpse of it, fluttering across the field and settling on the oak, and that his subconscious recognition of its identity had set in motion the proper mental mechanism to notify his upper consciousness of a fact in which it would naturally be much interested.

There may also be a subconscious intensification, or "hyperæsthesia," of other senses than that of sight. In all probability hyperæsthesia of the sense of hearing is sufficient to account for the dramatic central incident in the following story, told by a lady whose identity I am unable to reveal:

"I was living one summer in a little mining camp in the Rocky Mountains. Our house, a frame building, was some little distance from any other, at the top of a steep hill; the only disadvantage of this being the additional difficulty of getting water, which was an expensive commodity in the camp, as the adjacent mines had drained most of the wells.

"The house contained six rooms, all opening one out of another, my own room, with a dressing closet beyond, where my child slept, being at one end, and the front porch, which overlooked the valley, at the other.

"One evening, after my little girl was asleep, I lit a tiny night lamp, always left burning on a bracket in her room; and, leaving all doors and windows open, on account of the intense heat, went to sit on the front porch. I may have sat there half an hour, when my attention was caught by a great blazing light in the direction of the farthest houses. It appeared evident that one at least had taken fire, and the difficulty of getting water, and the hope that no children were in danger, flashed through my mind.

"While watching the rapidly growing glare, I heard a faint, crackling sound in my own house. It would not have disturbed me at any other time, as I only supposed that some smouldering piece of cedar in the kitchen stove had blazed up. But, with the present thought of fire in my mind, I went into the kitchen to look, and, glancing through the open doors as I passed, saw a volume of flame and smoke pouring from the child's room into mine.

"Thank God it was still possible to rush through and save her; and I carried her out in a blanket to prevent the scorch, for the room was only burning at one end; the side where the bed stood, though fearfully hot and suffocating, was not yet on fire, and, thanks to the timely warning, the water left in the barrels proved just enough to extinguish the flames before very much was destroyed.

"After all was quiet, I went back to the porch to look at that other burning house, feeling so thankful that my child was safe, and wondering if others were, also. But all was dark, and when I came to make inquiry next day, nothing was known in the camp of any such fire. Had it not been for my strange vision of it, which must have lasted fully ten minutes, I feel sure that my little girl would have been burned to death."[37]

There is a possibility, though only a possibility, that telepathy between mother and child may have had part in the production of this helpful hallucination. But hyperæsthesia of the sense of hearing seems to afford the likelier explanation, as also in numerous well-authenticated instances, in which railroad men, obeying an unaccountable impulse or hallucinatory monition, have taken action averting disastrous wrecks. A single illustrative example must suffice, a case called to the attention of the Society for Psychical Research by Mr. William H. Wyman, of Dunkirk, N. Y.:

"Some years ago my brother was employed on, and had charge as conductor and engineer of, a work train on the Lake Shore and Michigan Southern Railway, running between Buffalo and Erie. I often went with him to the gravel bank, where he had his headquarters, and returned on his train with him.

"On one occasion I was with him, and after the train of cars was loaded, we went together to the telegraph office to see if there were any orders, and to find out if the trains were on time, as we had to keep out of the way of all regular trains. After looking over the train reports, and finding them all on time, we started for Buffalo.

"As we approached Westfield station, running about twelve miles per hour, and when within about one mile of a long curve in the line, my brother all of a sudden shut off the steam, and, quickly stepping over to the fireman's side of the engine, he looked out of the cab window, and then to the rear of his train. Not discovering anything wrong, he put on steam, but almost immediately again shut it off, and gave the signal for brakes, and stopped.

"After inspecting the engine and train, and finding nothing wrong, he seemed very much excited, and for a short time he acted as if he did not know where he was or what to do. I asked what was the matter. He replied that he did not know; then, after looking at his watch and orders, he said that he felt that there was some trouble on the line of the road. I suggested that he had better run his train to the station and find out. He then ordered his flagman to go ahead around the curve, which was just ahead of us, and he would follow with the train.

"The flagman started and had barely time to flag an extra express train, with the general superintendent and others on board, coming full forty miles an hour. The superintendent inquired what he was doing there, and if he did not receive orders to keep out of the way of the extra. My brother told him that he had not received orders, and did not know of any extra train coming; that we had both examined the train reports before leaving the station. The train was then backed to the station, where it was found that no orders had been given."[38]

Incidents such as this are of not infrequent occurrence. By the superstitious

[37] Proceedings of the Society for Psychical Research, vol. xi, pp. 418-419.

[38] Proceedings of the Society for Psychical Research, vol. xi, p. 416.

they are regarded as weird and uncanny, and savoring of the spiritistic. In reality they are only exceptional exemplifications of a process which is ceaselessly taking place in all of us. There is no one who does not, every day, perform acts which he cannot consciously account for, and which, if closely inquired into, would be found similarly to take their rise in unnoticed subconscious impressions. For the matter of that, it is possible to train one-self to subconscious attention to selected impressions, even in sleep. A familiar illustration is the mother who, undisturbed by other sounds, awakens at the least cry of her infant. The same phenomenon is observable in the case of the conscientious medical nurse, who, no matter how profound her sleep, responds instantly to any movement by her patient. And, in the course of conversation not long ago, a physician said to me:

"As you know, my house is on a car line, and, besides the cars, there is much automobile and carriage traffic on my street for a large part of the night. Nothing of this breaks my rest. I sleep so soundly that a thunderstorm does not arouse me. Yet let the telephone bell begin to ring, and I am out of bed and have the receiver at my ear before the bell has ceased ringing."

I have myself, like a good many other people, found it possible to make the subconscious do the work of an alarm clock. That is to say, if, on going to bed, I mentally determine to wake at a certain hour, I invariably do so, and this although I am one of the deepest of sleepers. It matters not what hour I select, nor how late I retire the previous night, the mental sentinel whom I have placed on guard punctually notifies me when the appointed time arrives.

This goes to show, of course, that the subconscious is, to a certain extent, at any rate, amenable to conscious control and direction. That such control is highly desirable is evinced not merely by the facts reviewed above, but by others which we must next take under consideration—facts of altogether different import. For if, as we have seen, the subconscious is in many ways a docile and helpful auxiliary of the upper consciousness, it also contains within itself dire possibilities of unhappiness, suffering, disease, and even death.

CHAPTER VII

DISSOCIATION AND DISEASE

THE subconscious, I repeat, does not always exercise a helpful influence; there are times when it may impose upon us indescribable misery.

It is able to do this by virtue of the intimate relations existing between the mind and the body. At this late day it is scarcely necessary for me to undertake to demonstrate that the state of one's mind has a great deal to do with the health of one's body. What is not so generally known, and what all of us ought to know, is the further fact that many diseases are directly due to distressing mental states, and in such cases usually to subconscious mental states—that is to say, to thoughts and emotions of which the sufferer consciously has no knowledge. The same often holds good even with regard to maladies the symptoms of which are almost wholly if not altogether physical, and the causes of which one would naturally expect to find physical, likewise.

Indeed, ignorance of the tremendous rôle played by the subconscious in the causation of disease, has in the past been responsible for many medical shortcomings. Nor is the situation as yet much improved, although it is rapidly improving, thanks chiefly to the labors of a little group of scientific investigators known as psychopathologists, or medical psychologists, who have made it their special business to ascertain the different ways in which the subconscious may affect health adversely, and to devise methods for coping with mentally caused diseases.

These men are not "faith healers." They are not making any war on medicine. They are, in fact, themselves physicians, graduates of the best medical schools, of excellent standing in their profession, and seeking, above all things, to increase the usefulness and precision of medical science. Already, though their labors were begun only a few years ago, they have effected numerous cures of a seemingly miraculous character; but always they have effected them by utilizing natural laws which they have discovered by the rigorous processes of scientific experiment.

Of fundamental importance among these laws is one known as the law of dissociation. It might almost be called the law of forgotten memories, for to a large extent its workings depend on the interesting circumstance, to which attention has previously been drawn, that ideas which have faded from the conscious memory persist in the subconsciousness. As Pierre Janet, the distinguished Frenchman and most eminent of living psychopathologists, has tersely phrased it, "Nothing that goes into the human mind is ever really lost."

No matter how remote, past experiences, as I have shown in earlier chapters, can be recovered and recalled to mind by means of crystal-vision, automatic writing, or other psychological methods of "tapping the subconscious." Obviously we have here no absolute loss of memory, but merely a splitting off, or "dissociation," from the field of waking consciousness.

Now, while the memories thus dissociated and lying hidden in the subconscious usually exercise no appreciable effect other than in the molding of character, the enlargement of our store of knowledge, etc., there are conditions under which, in the case of persons predisposed by circumstances of heredity or environment, they may give rise to all manner of mental and physical ills.

A person, for instance, experiences a sudden fright. Time passes, the fright is completely forgotten, or, at most, vaguely remembered. But one day unmistakable, and sometimes exceedingly peculiar, symptoms of disease appear. The victim, it may be, suffers from a strange obsession or "fixed idea," or from a general "nervous breakdown," or from an actual paralysis of some bodily organ, or from the development of abdominal or other enlargements resembling true organic growths.

Whatever the symptoms, the mechanism of the puzzling malady is always the same. There has been an abnormal dissociation. The ideas connected with the original shock, although submerged beneath the threshold of consciousness—in a word, forgotten—remain vividly alive in the subconscious, to act as perpetual irritants of the nervous system and in time to give rise to the appearance of the symptoms of which the sufferer complains. Often, indeed, the dissociation is instantaneous, and the appearance of the disease symptoms equally rapid.

In either case, the resultant malady is purely psychical in its origin, and can be cured only by psychical, not by physical means. What is needed is to get at the dissociated mental states—the forgotten, disease-creating memories—and reassociate them with the upper consciousness, or root them out completely by means of "suggestions" skillfully applied.

This is no fanciful theory. It is the solidest kind of fact, repeatedly tested and verified. Time and again, patients pronounced incurable by competent physicians have been taken in hand by the psychopathologists and, once their disease has been definitely traced to some dissociation, have been restored to perfect health.

For the matter of that, of course, the same thing has been done to some extent by Christian Science healers and other irregular practitioners of "mental medicine." But the difference between all of these and the psychopathologists is just this—that the former apply the healing power of suggestion to all sorts of diseases, and without any adequate understanding of its laws and limitations, whereas the psychopathologists recognize that it is only one of several valuable medical methods, and that it is legitimately applicable only to certain maladies.

Experience has taught them, too, that even within its proper sphere of usefulness it often is of therapeutic value only after a searching scientific examination of the patient's subconsciousness has brought to light the particular dissociated states which have to be corrected before a cure can be wrought.

Nevertheless, the range of maladies susceptible of cure by psychopathological processes is marvelously wide, and it is no exaggeration to say that the discovery of the influence exercised by the subconscious in the causation of disease is one of the most vitally significant ever made in the history of medicine.

The truth of this may readily be shown by citing a few cases illustrating some of the manifold ways in which dissociation works havoc in the human organism, and the extreme ingenuity displayed by the skilled psychopathologist in overcoming its ravages.

There was brought one day to the Parisian hospital of the Salpêtrière, the world's greatest center of psychopathological investigation, a woman of forty, designated in the medical record of her case by the name of Justine. She was accompanied by her husband, who explained that he wished Doctor Janet to examine her because he feared that she had become insane. And, in fact, she presented the aspect of a veritable maniac. Her jet-black hair was flowing loosely over her shoulders, her eyes were fixed and glaring, her hands trembling, the muscles of her neck twitching, and she constantly made the most horrible grimaces. When Doctor Janet gently sought to question her, she buried her face in her hands, and cried:

"Oh, it is terrible to live thus! I am afraid, I am so afraid!"

"And of what, pray, are you afraid?" the physician asked.

"I am afraid of cholera."

"Is that all you are afraid of?"

"But surely it is quite enough."

Doctor Janet turned for an explanation to her husband, who shook his head despairingly, as he replied in an undertone:

"This is the way she has been for years, doctor, only lately she has grown much worse. She will scarcely eat anything, for fear of catching cholera. It is difficult to persuade her to stir from the house. She seems to think the air is full of cholera germs. She sees cholera in everything. Tell me, doctor, is my poor Justine mad? Must we be separated, she and I? Is it that she will have to spend the rest of her life in an asylum?"

"Leave her here a few days," said Doctor Janet, "and I can tell you better then."

Psychopathologists have invented some delicate tests for discriminating infallibly between true organic insanity, which in the present state of medical knowledge is quite incurable, and functional mental troubles due to dissociation. Applying these, Doctor Janet soon reached the conclusion that Justine was not really insane, and that her "phobia," or irrational fear, was due to some forgotten shock connected with the disease cholera.

But, closely though he questioned her, she could recall nothing of the sort. He then decided to try the effect of hypnotizing her, for, as all psychopathologists are aware, hypnotism, when it is possible to use it, is an unrivaled agency for recovering lost memories. Put into the hypnotic state, patients easily remember incidents in their past of which they have no conscious recollection when in the normal, waking state. It was thus with Justine, who proved to be most hypnotizable.

"I want you," Doctor Janet told her, after she had passed into deep hypnosis, "to try to remember whether at any time in your life you saw a person suffering from cholera, or one who had died from cholera."

"Why, certainly I did," she promptly replied, shuddering violently.

"When was it?"

"When I was a little girl—fifteen years old."

"Tell me the circumstances."

"My mother was very poor. She had to take all sorts of work. Sometimes she nursed sick people, and when they died she got them ready for burial. Once two people in our neighborhood died from cholera, and I helped her with the corpses. They made a frightful sight—one of them, at all events. It was the body of a man, naked, and all blue and green. Oh, frightful, frightful! What if I should catch the cholera? I shall catch it, I know I shall! Nothing can save me!"

Her voice rose in a shriek of terror, and Doctor Janet hastened to de-hypnotize her.

The situation was now perfectly clear to him. Evidently the sight of the corpse, "naked, and all blue and green," had so profoundly affected the impressionable girl as to cause a severe dissociation whereby all memory of the shocking episode had been blotted out of her consciousness, only to be subconsciously remembered in most minute detail.

To bring about a cure, to free her from the obsessing dread of cholera, it was necessary to remove the gruesome subconscious memory image, and Doctor Janet essayed to do this through suggestions given to her when she was again hypnotized.

"You will no longer think of this," he kept assuring her. "You will forget it, absolutely, permanently."

Day after day, for weeks, he hypnotized her, and reiterated similar commands. But she continued to be afflicted with her irrational fear, and it finally became certain that her subconscious recollection of the phobia-causing scene of twenty-five years before was too deeply rooted to be destroyed by direct attack. Instead, however, of abandoning the task as hopeless, Doctor Janet, with a shrewdness born of long experience, made a clever change in tactics.

"You insist," he said to the hypnotized Justine, "that you cannot help seeing in your mind's eye the corpse of the man who died. Very well, I have no objection to that. But hereafter you must see it decently clothed. So when it next appears to you, you will see it wearing a bright blue-and-green uniform, the uniform of a foreign military officer."

Happily, this suggestion "took," and Doctor Janet followed up his advantage by suggesting that the subconscious memory image which she regarded as that of a corpse was, in reality, the image of a living man. This suggestion likewise being successful, he set about getting rid of the idea "cholera," and its dire implications. Hypnotizing the patient as usual, he demanded:

"What is this 'cholera' that troubles you so much? Do you not understand that it is only the name of the fine gentleman in blue and green, whom you see marching up and down? He is a Chinese general, and his name is Cho Le Ra. Bear that well in mind."

Quite evidently there was nothing to inspire dread in the image of a picturesque Chinese officer, General Cho Le Ra. Little by little, as this artificial conception obtained firmer lodgment in Justine's subconsciousness, the baneful idea which it was intended to supplant faded away, and with its fading the abnormal fear diminished, until at length it entirely disappeared, greatly to her joy and the warm gratitude of her devoted husband.[39]

Other psychopathologists, following Doctor Janet's lead, have similarly used this method of substituting one subconscious idea for another. Doctor John E. Donley, a well-known neurologist of Providence, Rhode Island, and one of the few psychopathologists whom the United States has yet produced, was once consulted by a young man of thirty-two, who said to him:

"Doctor Donley, I hear you have been very successful in handling people troubled with foolish notions. I'm bothered with as foolish a notion as any one could possibly imagine. I simply can't bear to ride in a street-car with an odd number. Even-numbered cars give me no trouble at all, but if an odd-numbered car comes along, I've got to let it pass, no matter how great my hurry. My friends laugh at me, but I tell you it's no laughing matter. The thing has got on my nerves so that it is unbearable."

"How long have you been suffering in this way?" asked Doctor Donley.

"For years. Just when it began I can't remember.

"Is it only odd-numbered cars that affect you? How about odd-numbered houses, for instance?"

"No, no," answered the young man, "it isn't odd numbers in general. That doesn't bother me a bit. It's just when they're painted on street-cars."

"H'm," said Doctor Donley. "Ever been in a street-car accident?"

"Never."

"Ever seen one?"

"Not that I remember."

"You are quite sure as to that?"

"Quite."

"Have you any objection to my hypnotizing you?"

[39] This case and a number of other instances of forgotten terrors giving rise to disease-symptoms are discussed in detail in Doctor Janet's "Névroses et Idées Fixes."

"Not in the least, if it is likely to do me any good."

In another ten minutes the problem was solved. Doctor Donley from the outset had felt confident that the young man's phobia must be connected in some way with a street-car accident, and so it proved. Fourteen years earlier, when walking along the street, he had seen a car strike and seriously injure a child who unexpectedly came from behind a wagon. He had noticed at the time that the car bore the number two hundred and thirteen, and he remembered thinking to himself: "There is always bad luck in thirteen." The sight of the accident gave him a marked emotional shock, which, he said, upset him for several days.

All of this had long since passed from his waking memory, but was distinctly recalled during hypnosis. It was clear to Doctor Donley that the case was one of dissociation, and that the exciting cause of the young man's unreasonable dread of odd-numbered cars was based on a painfully vivid subconscious memory image of the consciously forgotten tragedy. Also, it was evident that before the dread could be overcome the distressing memory image would have to be eradicated.

To accomplish this, Doctor Donley resorted to the method of substitution, suggesting to the patient, while still under hypnotic influence, that he was quite mistaken in supposing that the street-car had seriously injured the little girl; that, on the contrary, it had scarcely touched her.

The result, after only eight days' treatment, was effectually to replace the painful memory image with one free from distressing associations. As by magic, the young man shook off his absurd phobia. No longer, when he had to take a car, did he stand on street corners, sometimes for an hour at a time, waiting anxiously for a car with an even number to appear.[40]

Bizarre as these cases must seem, they are actually typical of a widespread malady that causes an amount of suffering only appreciable by the sufferers themselves. In every land there are thousands of men and women afflicted with obsessions equally strange and equally distressing, yet amenable to treatment by the methods of psychopathology.

Often, in order to effect a cure, it is not necessary to make use of the roundabout device just described. Direct suggestion—a strongly negative command imposed in the hypnotic state—is frequently sufficient.

Often, besides, it is not necessary to use hypnotism at all, a cure resulting if only the psychopathologist can dig down to the root of the trouble, and, by recalling to conscious recollection the lost memory image, reassociate it with the rest of the contents of the upper consciousness.

Particularly interesting in this connection, as being illustrative also of an ingenious method of "mind tunnelling" nowadays frequently employed to get at forgotten memories, is a case reported by Doctor A. A. Brill, a New York psychopathologist. His patient was a young woman who applied to be treated for ex-

[40] This case and several others similarly illustrative of the disease-creating power of emotional disturbances are discussed by Doctor Donley in "Psychotherapeutics," a book of composite authorship.

treme nervousness. She had been perfectly well until three months before, when, she said, she had begun to suffer from a complication of disorders, including insomnia, loss of appetite, constant headache, irritability, and stomach trouble. No physical cause for her condition could be detected, and Doctor Brill suspected that it was due to some secret anxiety, but the patient earnestly assured him that she "had nothing on her mind."

To get at the facts which he suspected she was consciously or unconsciously concealing from him, Doctor Brill decided to make use of what is known as the "association-reaction method of mental diagnosis," a cumbersome and formidable term for a really simple process.

Everybody knows that if a man is suddenly asked a question bearing on matters which personally concern him and which he is anxious to keep entirely to himself, he is apt to "react" to the question in a way that will betray the true state of affairs. He may blush or stammer before replying, may reply evasively, may find it impossible to reply at all. If he is a man of uncommon self-control, and not to be taken off his guard, the reply may come smoothly enough, and to all appearance without hesitation. Nevertheless, experiment has shown that, even in such cases, there is an appreciable difference in the time, if not in the character, of the replies he makes to emotion-arousing questions, as compared with the time it takes him to reply to questions that have no special significance to him. The same holds good in the case of questions evoking within him memories—albeit perhaps wholly subconscious memories—of happenings that may be no longer, but once were, of keen emotional import to him.

Out of the discovery of this fact the association-reaction method has been evolved. The specialist using it reads slowly to his patient a list of one hundred words or more, and requests him, as he hears each, to respond with the first word that comes into his mind. Seemingly the list of stimulus words is chosen at random; actually it is so constructed that some of the words are likely to stir into activity the subconscious memories of which the physician is in search. If they do this the fact will be disclosed in the time of his reaction-words—the words he utters in reply—as measured by a chronoscope or stop-watch; or in their character, as noted down by the specialist.

Of course, it is necessary for the physician to select words having, or likely to have, emotional significance to the particular patient; and as a guide in the selection, strange though it may seem, nothing is more useful than the patient's dreams. For it has been definitely established that dreams are far from being the haphazard products of imagination they are generally supposed to be; that on the contrary, no matter how trivial or nonsensical they seem, they always have an emotional foundation corresponding with some present or past reality; and that usually they mask matters of distinct significance to the dreamer.

As a preliminary, then, in the treatment of his nervous patient, Doctor Brill asked her to write out her dreams and bring them to him.

"But," she said, "I never dream, except when I am troubled by indigestion, and then my dreams are so absurd that they are not worth telling."

"Never mind," was his reply. "Whenever you do happen to have a dream, report it to me."

Laughingly she promised to comply, and one day brought him the following:

"I dreamed that I was in a lonely country place and was anxious to reach my home, but could not get there. Every time I made a move there was a wall in the way—it looked like a street full of walls. My legs were as heavy as lead; I could only walk very slowly as if I were very weak or very old. Then there was a flock of chickens, but that seemed to be in a crowded city street, and they—the chickens—ran after me, and the biggest of all said something like: 'Come with me into the dark.'"

"There," she said, "that is my dream, and if you can make head or tail of it, it is more than I can. It is so ridiculous that I am ashamed to tell it."

But Doctor Brill was already at work drawing up a test list, with the more striking words of the dream sprinkled through it. Twice he read the list to her, noting not only the time of her responses, but also their character.

He was immediately impressed by the fact that certain of the dream words—such as "chicken," "street," and "dark" had caused a noticeable time variation; and that she had also given in her responses words that would not ordinarily be associated with the test words. Especially peculiar was the association of "mystery" and "marriage" with the word "dark." The suspicion formed in his mind that a disappointment in love might be at the bottom of all her disease symptoms. But he did not at once give voice to this idea; instead, he sought to obtain corroboration from her own lips without her appreciating his purpose, by means of another method of "mind tunnelling" known as the method of free association.

"I want you," he said to her, "to concentrate your attention on the word 'chicken,' and state the thoughts that come to you in connection with it."

Her reply, given after a few moments of silent meditation, was:

"I remember now that I could see only the biggest chicken; all the others seemed blurred; it was unusually big and had a very long neck and it spoke to me. The street in which I saw it recalls where I used to go to school—the block was always crowded with school children."

She paused, and began to blush and laugh.

"Go on," said Doctor Brill encouragingly. "What next?"

"Why, it recalls the happy school days when I was young and had no worries. I even had a beau, a boy who attended the same school. We used to meet after school hours and walk home together. He was lanky and thin, and the girls used to tease me about him. Whenever they saw him coming, they said: 'Belle, here comes your chicken.' That was his nickname among the boys."

Stopping suddenly, she exclaimed:

"Doctor Brill, it couldn't be possible that the chicken with the long neck, that I saw in my dream, was my old beau!"

"It begins to look very much like it," he smiled. "Have you seen him lately?"

"Not for months."

"And before then?"

Little by little the whole story came out. They had kept up their acquaintance after the school days were long gone. Three times he had asked her to marry him, but each time she had refused, because although she "liked" him she was not at all sure that she "loved" him. At last she had decided that the next time he proposed she would accept. But he had not proposed again. And shortly before she became ill she had heard that he was paying attentions to another young lady.

"I take it," interposed Doctor Brill, "that he is not so well off as he might be, and that this had something to do with your refusing to marry him."

"What makes you say that?"

"In your dream I note that you state: 'Every time I made a move there was a wall in the way; it looked like a street full of walls.' A street full of walls might easily signify Wall Street—hence money. That has been the real obstacle, has it not?"

She confessed that he was right.

He then explained that the one great cause of her ills was her insistent, if subconscious, brooding over the disappointment she had experienced, and that her cure depended upon her ability to overcome this mental attitude. Realizing for the first time, as a result of the dream analysis, that she was really in love with the man she had three times declined to wed, she soon solved the problem. Only a hint was needed to transform him into a suitor once more, and within a very few months they were happily married.[41]

Sometimes direct questioning is sufficient to enable the physician to get at the underlying mental cause of trouble. Take, for example, another case successfully treated by Doctor Donley.

The patient was a woman of thirty-five who was troubled by a constant and involuntary hacking, which sounded as though she were trying to clear her throat. Drugs, local applications, and electricity had been tried at intervals during more than four years, but to no purpose. On inquiry, it was found that the trouble had set in about five years before, when the patient, who was a mill hand, had suffered from a sore throat. The physician whom she then consulted told her that she had a bad case of tonsilitis, and that her tonsils would have to be burned out.

Greatly frightened, she had hurried home, refusing to submit to the operation. In a few days the tonsilar symptoms disappeared, and she returned to work. But she was attacked a second time three weeks later, and visited another doctor, to be informed that her tonsils were so badly diseased that it would be well to have them removed by cutting.

Again she refused to submit to an operation, but the fear of cutting, added to her previous fear, now revived, of burning out her tonsils, threw her into a highly

[41] Doctor Brill has reported and discussed this case in his recently published "Psychoanalysis," pp. 48-54.

nervous state. She then began to experience an unpleasant stinging, tickling feeling in her throat, which she tried to remove by hacking. As the tickling continued, the hacking became more and more frequent, and by the time she came under Doctor Donley's observation had taken on the character of a "tic," or uncontrollable muscular movement.

These facts in the early history of the case, the patient herself remembered only vaguely. But she confessed that she was still tormented by a haunting fear of a possible future burning or cutting of her tonsils. Finding her exceedingly suggestible, Doctor Donley made no attempt to hypnotize her. He merely requested her to close her eyes, remain perfectly passive, and listen attentively to him.

"She was then told, with much emphasis," he says, in describing the treatment, "that her tonsils were perfectly healthy, that no cutting or burning ever was or ever would be required; that the tickling sensation in her throat arose from the constant fixation of attention upon this part; that she would feel no more desire to hack because her supposed reason for hacking had ceased to exist, and finally, that when she should open her eyes she would feel better than she had in a good many years.

"Much emphasis was placed upon this feeling of health, because it was desired to leave her on the crest of a pleasurable emotion, which of itself has a very great suggestive value. What had been predicted in her regard actually occurred. When she sat up, her tic had disappeared, and she expressed herself as feeling quite grateful and happy. The treatment lasted an hour, and except for two slight recurrences easily removed by waking suggestion, this patient has had no further difficulty."[42]

Unfortunately, such an easy solution of problems like this is comparatively rare, particularly when, as in this instance, a physical trouble is superadded to the mental. Often—a fact which cannot be emphasized too strongly—it happens that, in dissociational cases, physical symptoms so far predominate as to lead to totally wrong diagnosis, even by experienced physicians. This results, as was hinted above, from the power inherent in subconscious "fixed ideas" of producing an endless variety of disturbances simulating true organic diseases, it may be diseases remediable only through surgical operations.

As a consequence, innumerable operations have been performed on patients who should have been given, not surgical but psychopathological treatment. I have in mind as I write a case of this kind that was called to my attention by a friend who participated in the lamentable affair.

A middle-aged woman entered one of the Boston hospitals and complained of severe abdominal pains, which she attributed to cancer of the stomach or intestines. She was obviously greatly frightened, and suffering intense agony. A diagnosis of appendicitis was made, and an immediate operation deemed imperative.

But, to the surprise of the surgeons, the appendix was found to be in a normal condition. At once they directed their attention to the other abdominal organs, examining them one by one. None showed any sign of disease. Finally, with a rueful

[42] Quoted from "Psychotherapeutics: A Symposium," p. 152.

smile, one of the surgeons straightened up, and, touching a finger to his head, said:

"The trouble with this poor woman, gentlemen, is here, not in the region that we have been exploring. But we should not undeceive her. We will remove the appendix, on general principles, and that will probably be all that is needed to cure the trouble in her head."

Under the circumstances, it was excellent advice. But how much better it would have been for the unfortunate woman, whose life was thus endangered by the surgeon's knife, if it had been recognized from the beginning that her malady was only a "hysterical simulation" of the symptoms of appendicitis. Some day, when physicians generally make themselves acquainted with the diagnostic methods of psychopathology, blunders like this will be, as they ought to be, most exceptional.

In point both of diagnosis and treatment, again, psychopathological knowledge is indispensable to the correct handling of such cases as the following, reported by Doctor Janet.[43] It is, I am ready to concede, an unusual case, but it is unusual only because it presents a complex of symptoms commonly found singly or in simpler combination.

It would be impossible to estimate with any accuracy the number of persons who, afflicted only in scant degree like this poor Marcelle, have been obliged to drag out an existence worse than death, either in the care of their friends or immured in an institution, simply because their medical attendants, ignorant of the workings of the law of dissociation, have been unable to fathom the true nature of their ills and adopt adequate curative measures.

Marcelle, as Doctor Janet calls her, was only nineteen years old when she began to astonish her relatives by developing what they were at first disposed to regard as nothing but an eccentric form of laziness. She would constantly ask them to give her objects—a book, her crochet work, a plate—which she could easily have got for herself by stretching out her hand and picking them up. To all expostulations, she would calmly reply:

"I can't help it. I can't use my hands as I once did, and that's all there is to it."

"You can't use your hands! What nonsense! You can use them to eat with, well enough, and you are crocheting most of the time."

"Oh, but that's different."

"What's the difference? Tell us."

But Marcelle could not, or would not, tell them, and from joking with her the family soon passed to a state of wrath, endeavoring in every way to overcome her "stupid obstinacy." Their anger in turn gave way to fear, when, one night, noticing a glimmer of light in her room, they entered, and found her standing, fully dressed, before the bed.

"But what is this!" they exclaimed, in amazement. "Why don't you get your clothes off and go to bed?"

[43] In "Névroses et Idées Fixes," vol. i, pp. 1-68.

"Because," she cried, "I can't undress!"

And, all arguments proving vain, it was necessary for her sister to disrobe her as though she were a tiny child. Next day a consultation was held, and it was decided to take her to the Salpêtrière.

"She doesn't seem insane," her mother explained, when applying to have her admitted. "She talks sensibly about most things. Can it be that she is really suffering from some kind of paralysis?"

"Most assuredly," was the reply, "and we will do our best to discover what it is and cure it."

This turned out to be no easy matter. Doctor Janet, into whose care she came, had no difficulty in determining that the specific malady which afflicted her was an extreme form of "aboulia," a disease involving temporary paralysis of the will, and thereby preventing all muscular movement. But it was one thing to make a diagnosis, and another to effect a cure.

Presently, too, indications of mental disturbance developed. Doctor Janet had discovered that by distracting her attention he could induce her to rise, extend her hands, and perform other acts that were impossible to her when she concentrated her attention on them. He utilized this as an argument to try and persuade her that she could always control her limbs if she only made sufficient effort.

"But you are quite wrong," she calmly informed him. "I have not left my chair, I have not put out my hand."

"Most assuredly you have. You know very well I did not give you that piece of crochet work. How, then, does it come into your hands?"

"I did not pick it up."

"Who did, then?"

"Somebody else—somebody acting in me."

A little later arose another complication. She refused to eat, and it became necessary to administer food to her forcibly. She kept saying to herself:

"You must die, you must die as soon as possible. You must not eat, you have no need of eating. You must not speak, you have no voice, you are paralyzed."

"Why do you say this?" Doctor Janet one day asked her.

"Why do I say what?"

He repeated her words.

"But I have said nothing of the sort."

"Oh, yes, you have."

"No, no, no—it was not I; it was somebody else acting in me."

Again that phrase—"somebody else acting in me." Greatly impressed, Doctor Janet threw her into deep hypnosis. Now, an unexpected and most pathetic passage of personal history came to light. A year before, Marcelle had had a secret love affair, her lover had deserted her, she had determined to commit suicide. Failing to do this, she had, none the less—overwhelmed by the shock of the desertion, and giving herself wholly to grief and chagrin, which she felt obliged to allow no one to perceive—gradually passed into a dissociated, dreamlike state, in which she subconsciously pictured herself to herself either as no longer existing or as about to perish.

Hence her "aboulia," hence the "somebody else acting in me," hence the refusal to take food. To Doctor Janet the situation was now almost as clear as the light of day—so, likewise, was the course which he would need to follow to restore the sufferer to her "real self," and rid her of all disease symptoms.

The dissociation, to put it briefly, had in this case been so complete as to cause an actual disruption of the sense of personality. Nor is this malady of "loss of personality" as rare as one might be tempted to think. I could mention many cases not unlike that of Marcelle's, and some far surpassing it in astounding developments. There is, for example, the singular case of BCA. But this is so remarkable, so weirdly fascinating, and so instructive that it deserves to be treated, as I shall treat it in the next chapter, entirely by itself.

CHAPTER VIII

THE SINGULAR CASE OF BCA

DURING his long career as a specialist in the treatment of nervous and mental diseases, Doctor Morton Prince, the celebrated Boston psychopathologist, has been called upon to deal with many puzzling human riddles, and to solve mysteries which, in their way, have been quite as complicated and baffling as any that ever taxed the ingenuity of that most ingenious of story-book detectives, Mr. Sherlock Holmes. In fact, some of the problems laid before the New England specialist surpass even the most astonishing of the adventures of Sherlock Holmes, thus proving once more that truth is stranger than fiction. This particularly applies to the BCA affair.

In the beginning, however, there was nothing in the BCA affair to suggest to Doctor Prince that it had features which would test to the utmost his psychopathological skill. It opened in a prosaic, matter-of-fact way, with the arrival at his office of a young woman who wished to be treated for what she described as a "nervous breakdown." The story she told was a sad one, but he had heard many quite like it before, and it did not impress him as involving anything out of the ordinary.

"My trouble," she said, in describing the evolution of her malady, "began when my husband was attacked with an incurable disease. For four years my life was altogether given up to caring for him, striving to make him as comfortable as possible, and endeavoring to conceal from him my grief and anxiety. You can imagine the strain put upon me all that time. Finally he died, under circumstances that caused me a great shock.

"Within less than a week after his death, I lost twenty pounds in weight. For nearly three months I ate scarcely anything, and did not average more than three or four hours' sleep out of the twenty-four. I was depressed, overwhelmed; felt that I had lost all that made life worth living; and, in short, wished to die. I became highly nervous, tired easily, and suffered almost constantly from headaches.

"This went on for many months. Then there came a period of temporary recovery. Strangely enough, it followed an occurrence that brought to me suddenly a realization that my position in life was entirely changed, that I was quite alone, desolate, and helpless. For a few minutes these ideas flashed through my mind, and then all seemed changed. I no longer minded what, a moment before, had caused me so much distress; and, what is more, I immediately began to improve in health, until I was able to mingle with my friends, take long walks, go driving, and really enjoy life as I had formerly done. Alas, there soon was a relapse, and now I am feeling worse than ever."

Listening to her recital, and examining carefully her mental and physical condition, Doctor Prince felt justified in assuring her that there was nothing seriously the matter, and that he would ere long have her on the highway to health. In fact, he regarded her case as one presenting "the ordinary picture of so-called neurasthenia, characterized by persistent fatigue and the usual somatic symptoms, and by moral doubts and scruples"; and planned a course of treatment which he expected would speedily result in a cure. It was, to describe it briefly, treatment by hypnotic suggestion—a method often employed by psychopathologists in handling cases of neurasthenia, for they have discovered that it is perfectly feasible to "suggest away" the fatigue, insomnia, and other symptoms connected with this widespread and distressing malady.

The use of hypnotism in the present instance, though, was attended by consequences vastly different from any Doctor Prince had anticipated, since it revealed to him that his patient was, in reality, suffering from something infinitely more serious than ordinary neurasthenia, and infinitely more difficult to overcome. Put into the hypnotic state, her ills, to Doctor Prince's amazement, disappeared as though by a miracle. Her whole expression was altered. She looked, and declared that she felt, entirely well. It was hard to believe that this radiant, vigorous, brightly smiling woman was the one who had entered his office so short a time before, a typical nervous wreck, her features haggard and careworn, her eyes dull and heavy, her hands trembling. And, most astonishing of all, the hypnotized patient herself insisted that, in a very literal sense, she was not the same person.

The tone, the language, the manner—all were changed. Struck with sudden apprehension, Doctor Prince quickly brought her out of hypnosis. Immediately there was another transformation, and she was neurasthenic once more, without the slightest remnant of the strength, independence, and self-assertiveness she had just been displaying. Nor, although she was sharply questioned, could she remember anything she had said while hypnotized; still, this proved nothing, for it is seldom that what goes on during hypnosis is recalled in the waking state.

But, comparing her latest declarations with her prior account of the course her malady had run, Doctor Prince could not help asking himself whether she might not actually be a victim of what is technically designated "total dissociation of personality," whether the second emotional shock of which she had spoken, acting on a system already disorganized by the severe and prolonged strain imposed upon her by her husband's illness, might not have resulted in a psychical upheaval so catastrophic as to involve the disintegration of her ego, or "self," and the creation of a secondary self markedly differing from her original personality.

In such an event, the period of temporary recovery would, indeed, represent a period when the secondary self had obtained at least partial control of the patient's organism; and it was quite conceivable that there might come a time when, momentarily, at any rate, the secondary self would become wholly dominant. In that case, the young woman's plight would be appalling, for she would be in ignorance of all she said and did while in the secondary state. This was precisely what occurred.

Only a few days after she had first visited him, she came into Doctor Prince's office in a greatly excited condition.

"Doctor," she cried, "the strangest, the most inexplicable thing has happened to me! This morning, after breakfast, I went up-stairs, intending to lie down for a time, as I felt so utterly exhausted. I think I fell asleep, but am not sure. I do know, though, that two hours afterward I found myself standing in the post-office, about to mail to you a letter which I am certain I did not write, but which is plainly in my handwriting. It is such a queer letter, too, for it speaks of matters of which I know nothing, and even refers to me as though I were somebody else, and somebody else were I. What does this mean? What does it mean?"

And, in a day or so, she had an even stranger story to relate.

"Yesterday afternoon," she said, "I went for a walk, not because I wanted to, but because you had told me that I ought to take some exercise. I returned home about four o'clock, and went straight to my room. I remember nothing of what then happened until, in the evening, I suddenly became aware that I was at a gay dinner party, drinking wine—which is contrary to my principles—and, what was far worse, smoking a cigarette. Never in my life had I done such a thing, and my humiliation at the discovery was deep and keen.

"I assure you, on my honor, that I have not the least recollection of accepting an invitation to dine out, of dressing for dinner, or of leaving the house to attend the party. Everything is a blank to me from the moment I went to my room, in the afternoon, until I came to my senses, several hours afterward, to find a lively group about me, a wineglass at my plate, and a half-smoked cigarette in my fingers. Tell me, Doctor Prince, am I going insane?"

The physician hastened to reassure her, but nevertheless he felt seriously alarmed. It was evident that she was in a thoroughly dissociated condition, and that she had become, so to speak, a battleground on which was to be fought out the weirdest and most uncanny of conflicts—a duel between two separate selves for absolute supremacy in the use of the organs of her body.

Further, it soon developed that the advantage would lie with the secondary self—which Doctor Prince called her B self—because, although her ordinary, or A self, suffered from amnesia, or loss of memory, regarding her actions when in the B state, the B self had a memory extending over both states. The mental agony growing out of this recurring forgetfulness on A's part may readily be imagined. As the patient herself has since expressed it, in an autobiographical account written at Doctor Prince's request:[44]

"The amnesia made life very difficult; indeed, except for the help you gave

[44] This autobiographical account was first published in the Journal of Abnormal Psychology. Afterwards it was brought out in book form by Richard G. Badger, the Boston publisher, under the title, "My Life as a Dissociated Personality," and with an introduction by Doctor Prince. It is an account well worth reading by all students of psychology.

me, I think it would have been impossible, and that I should have gone truly mad. How can I describe or give any clear idea of what it is to wake suddenly, as it were, and not to know the day of the week, the time of the day, or why one is in a given position? I would come to myself as A, perhaps on the street, with no idea of where I had been, or where I was going; fortunate if I found myself alone, for if I was carrying on a conversation I knew nothing of what it had been; fortunate, indeed, in that case, if I did not contradict something I had said, for, as B, my attitude toward all things was quite the opposite of that taken by A."

Picture to yourself, my reader, how you would feel if, for a few hours almost every day, and sometimes for whole days at a stretch, you became virtually nonexistent, yet were made to realize, from what your friends told you, that a something or a somebody had taken possession of your organism, and was veritably acting in your place, and in a way utterly unlike your natural self. This was the state of affairs with Doctor Prince's luckless patient. In moods, tastes, points of view, habits of thought, and controlling ideas, her secondary personality was the very reverse of that which had been dominant when she first sought medical advice.

There even were pronounced physical differences. Whenever she was in the A state, she was extremely neurasthenic, being afflicted now by one, now by another, of the multifarious functional disturbances that accompany neurasthenia, and being exhausted by the slightest effort. A walk of a few hundred yards would be almost enough to prostrate her.

In the B state, on the contrary, she did not know the meaning of the word "pain," and was seemingly incapable of feeling fatigue. She would walk for miles without experiencing the slightest distress, was constantly on the go, and appeared to be in every way an exceptionally robust, healthy woman. Thus, physically, she was—as B—a decided improvement over herself as A. But with respect to psychical differences it was altogether another matter.

In the A state, she was kind, considerate of others, self-sacrificing, animated by a keen sense of, and devotion to, duty; profoundly stirred by any tale of sorrow or suffering, and most conscientious—if anything, overconscientious, being tortured at times in an extraordinary degree by moral doubts. In the B state, she was selfish, thoughtless, and cold; one might almost say devoid of human feeling. Here is the way she herself has put it:

"As B, I felt no emotion, except that of pleasure, using the word pleasure as meaning a 'good time'—social gayety, driving, motoring, walking, boating, etc.; but my enjoyment of these things was very keen. As B, I was always the gayest of the company, but for people I cared nothing. The little acts of affection which we all perform in daily home life I never thought of. The habit of shaking hands with one's friends, kissing or embracing those nearer and dearer, had no meaning to me. Ordinarily, I think, when one shakes hands with a friend, one feels the individuality of the person, more or less, and the clasp of hands means something; but, as B, it meant no more to me than clasping a piece of wood, and the acts of shaking hands, embracing, or kissing were all alike—it made no difference to me which I did—one meant just as much as the other. This lack of feeling applied only to people, for I loved the outside world; the trees, the water, the sky, and the wind seemed to be a very part of myself. But the emotions by which as A I was torn to shreds, as B I did not feel at all."

In still further contrast, this most remarkable young woman, when in the B state, was giddy, irresponsible, and frivolous. In the A state, she was most serious-minded and intellectual, being fond of reading such excellent literature as the works of Shakespeare, Hugo, Ibsen, Tolstoi, and Maeterlinck. All this, B found very tiresome, and cared only for the lightest kind of fiction, when she read at all.

In matters of dress and social pleasures, A and B were also diametrically opposed. A believed that she ought to wear black; B, who seems never to have given a thought to the dead husband, detested black, and, on the other hand, had a really abnormal liking for white. So that, as the two selves alternated in control, the strange spectacle was presented of the same woman at one moment arrayed in deep mourning, at another dressed in some light, bright gown.

To cap the climax, B took a malicious pleasure in tormenting her other self in many ways. She made engagements which she knew that, as A, she would not like to keep; she cultivated friendships with people with whom, as A, she had little desire to associate; she was wastefully extravagant, freely spending on useless articles money which, as A, she had been carefully hoarding against a rainy day; she indulged in innumerable petty, but annoying, practical jokes at A's expense.

For example: A would often wake in the morning to find on her pillow or dressing-table notes advising her jeeringly to "cheer up," to "weep no more," and not to "bother Doctor Prince so much." These notes she herself had written during the night, having changed to the B state while she slept, awakened as B, risen, and penned the notes, and then returned to bed, to fall asleep once more, and, in the morning, awake as A, with no memory of what she had done since retiring.

The flood of notes continuing, she began to destroy them unread, hoping that this would discourage B's malicious activity. It only made matters worse, for B now began to affix the notes to the center of her mirror, pasting above them inscriptions warning her to be sure to read them, and declaring that they contained—as they sometimes did—information of importance to her.

But the best idea of the topsyturvy, kaleidoscopic, almost incredible life led by this woman with a double existence may be given by quoting a few extracts from a diary kept jointly by the two personalities, at Doctor Prince's suggestion. Unique as a record of human experiences, it had a distinctly practical value, for it enabled A to keep track of what she had been doing while B was in control. B, of course, had no need of it for this purpose, since, as was said, she did not suffer from loss of memory, like A. The extracts quoted are not always in chronological order; but, for the present purpose, that is unimportant:

"I am here again to-night, B, I am. I may as well tell all I have done, I suppose. For one thing, I had a facial massage—there is no need of being a mass of wrinkles. I know A doesn't care how she looks, but I do. The Q's spent the evening here, and I smoked a cigarette. Now, A, don't go and tell Doctor Prince; you don't have to tell him everything—you do it, though. I *must* have a little fun."

"I have struggled through another day. B has told what she did. How *can* I bear it? How explain? I am so humiliated, so ashamed. Why should I do things which so mortify my pride? Quite ill all day. I am, as usual, paying for B's 'fun.' It is not to be borne."

"A terrible day—one of the worst for a long time. I *cannot* live this way; it is not to be expected. I am so confused. I have lost so much time now that I can't seem to catch up. What is the end to be? What will become of me?"

"A was used up, and had to stay in bed all the morning, but I came about one o'clock, and Mrs. X asked me to motor down to Z. Had a gorgeous ride, and got home at seven, nearly famished, for A had eaten nothing all day—she lives on coffee and somnos—nice combination!—steak and French fried for mine, please."

"Good gracious! How we fly around! A has been ill all the day, could not sleep last night. I hope he [Doctor Prince] won't send for us, for he will put a quietus on me, and, as things are now, I am gaining on A. Had a gay evening—no discussions of religion or psychology, no dissecting of hearts and souls while I am in the flesh."

"I wonder if A is really dead—for good and all? It seems like it. The thought rather frightens me some way, as if I had lost my balance wheel. She wants to die, she really does, for she thinks it to herself all the time. I wish I were myself alone, and neither A nor B; I cannot bear to hear A groan, she cannot bear my glee."

"Such a day! A got away from me for a little while, and tried to write a letter to Doctor Prince. It was a funny-looking letter, for I kept saying to her: 'You cannot write, you cannot move your hand,' but she had enough will power to write some, and direct it. The effort used her up, however, and I came, and the letter was not mailed."

"I am too much bewildered to write. I have succeeded in writing Doctor Prince. If I can only mail it! Oh, but I am tired! Such an awful struggle!"

"Another queer thing happened to-day. I have not been to the cemetery for a long time, so started to go there. I had gone only a little way when I began to feel that I could not go on. I do not mean that I did not wish to, but that I could not easily move my feet in that direction. It was as if some physical force was restraining me, or like walking against a heavy wind. I kept on, however, and finally reached the entrance; but farther I found it impossible to go. I was *held*—could not move my feet one inch in that direction. I set my will, and said to myself: 'I *will* go, I *can* go, and I will!' But I could not do it. I began to feel very tired—exhausted—and turned back. As soon as I turned away, I had no trouble in walking, but I was very tired."

These last paragraphs refer to a phase of the case which was, from the standpoint both of the patient and Doctor Prince, one of its most serious and mysterious features. Although B, try as she might—and she undoubtedly tried hard enough—could not permanently oust the A self, and had to be content with manifesting as an alternating personality, it was none the less the fact that, even when A was uppermost, B was able to exercise, from some subconscious region, a certain amount of influence, often impelling A to do things contrary to her inclinations.

The consequence was that A suffered fearfully from what seemed to be aboulia, or paralysis of will, somewhat similar to that experienced by Doctor Pierre Janet's patient, Marcelle, described in the preceding chapter. The cemetery episode was only one of many incidents, when, overpowered by some force she could not understand, and which was actually the superior will of B, she was unable to carry out projects she wished to execute, or was made to perform acts not at all to her liking.

The diary is full of allusions to this subconscious mastery of A by B. Scores of times, B influenced her to read some particular book she—B—wished to read, or to go out for a walk when she—A—wished to remain at home. Naturally A began to consider herself changeable and weak-minded.

"One day," B writes, "it was raining and she did not want to go out, but I felt that I could not stay in the house another minute. So I willed that she should go to walk, and she changed her clothes and went out. She thought: 'What nonsense this is to go out in this rain! I wish I knew what I wanted to do five minutes at a time.' She would think: 'I guess I will go to walk.' And then she would think: 'No, I don't want to go out in all this rain.' Then, in a few minutes: 'I believe I *will* go to walk,' etc. And finally she went, more for peace of mind than anything else."

Frequently, moreover, the subconscious willing to affect A's conduct, resulted in completely effacing A, and allowing B to reëmerge spontaneously, in full control.

Thus, there was a dinner party which B was anxious to attend, but while A was dressing she—A—decided she would not go, and started across the room to telephone and say she would not be present. At once B subconsciously began to think: "I want to go," "You must go." And poor A first became very much confused, then faded away entirely, with the result that the telephone message was not sent, and B was free to attend the party, and enjoy another of the "good times" that meant so much to her.

Where A suffered most of all by reason of this subtle power of B to influence her actions, lay in the difficulty she had in communicating with Doctor Prince, and in going to him for treatment. B well knew that her career would come to an end the moment Doctor Prince succeeded in reassociating his patient's disintegrated personality, and she fought desperately to preserve her existence, repeatedly preventing A, as mentioned in the extracts quoted from the diary, from telephoning to Doctor Prince, writing to him, or visiting him; all of which greatly increased A's confusion, misery, and unhappiness.

But, as it chanced, although Doctor Prince was earnestly desirous of effectually and forever suppressing B, he was not at all desirous of doing this for A's sake; and was, in fact, as anxious to get rid of A as he was to get rid of B.

For, to inject a new complication into this most complicated affair, he had by this time discovered that A had no more right to consideration than B, since A no more than B represented the patient's normal personality. His searching study of the case—the duel between A and B lasted a year or more—had convinced him that there had been not a single, but a double, dissociation of personality; and that the normal self, in consequence first of the shock occasioned by the husband's illness and death, and afterward of the shock that brought the B personality to the fore, had been violently relegated to some obscure department of the patient's subconsciousness, where, however, it assuredly was existent, and where it was an intensely interested, if helpless, spectator of the struggle being waged for control by the two usurping selves.

To recall this lost self, which he designated as C, was Doctor Prince's paramount object; and, after many months of weary and futile effort, he ultimately succeeded. One day, after he had plunged his patient into deep hypnosis, he saw that she had undergone a striking change. Physically she seemed much as in the B state, though not so boisterously vigorous; mentally she was like A, thoughtful and intellectual, but happily devoid of the vacillation and morbid overconscientiousness that had made A's life a misery to herself, and most difficult to all who came in contact with her.

Questioned, she showed that in this new state she possessed a complete memory for both the A and the B states, and was closer to normal than either. In Doctor Prince's mind, no doubt remained—he had found C, the missing self, the self which, after nearly two years of exile, had promise of coming once more into its own.

It had yet to be reëstablished in sovereignty—no easy task, as the event proved. Not many hours after its first emergence, B once more put in an appearance, wrathful, vehement, and defiant, angrily challenging Doctor Prince to suppress it if he could. Then came A, and soon a momentary return of C, quickly put to flight, however, by the still powerful will of B. In short, the conflict now became triangular, with B and C active opponents, and A a participant because she could not help herself.

The invaluable diary affords a clear view of the chaos that prevailed, and of the increasing effectiveness of Doctor Prince's vigorous reënforcement, by hypnotic suggestion, of the claims of C. We find, for instance, B lamenting, after several days' banishment:

"Well, once more I am permitted to write in this diary. After we got home, C went to pieces. I never saw such a lot! And then poor old A came again, in anguish, wringing of hands, finally tears. Then, thank goodness, I came myself! I *cannot* see why Doctor Prince would rather have that *emotional, hysterical* set than to have *me*! It passes comprehension. I know *everything, always*, and they know only a few things for a few minutes."

The note of woe and panic sounded here was amply justified. Little by little, A and B became less in evidence, until at length they were heard from no more, and C—the normal self—was left dominant, with a complete restoration to physical as well as mental health.

But, the reader may well ask, what does all this mean? Can there really be more than one self, one personality, in human beings? If so, what are we? What is the true nature of man? These are questions that cannot be avoided, and in my next and closing chapter I will make some attempt to answer them.

CHAPTER IX

THE LARGER SELF

IT is barely fifty years since the problem of supreme interest to mankind—the problem of the nature, possibilities, and destiny of man—began to be studied in a really scientific way; yet in that half century more progress has been made toward its solution than in all the previous thousands of years that have elapsed since man first asked himself: What am I? What are my capabilities? Shall I be, after I have ceased to exist here on earth?

Armed with instruments of the most delicate precision, devising novel methods for exploring the body and the mind in their mutual ramifications, modern investigators have thrown a flood of new and largely unexpected light on the great questions at issue, and have opened vistas of hope and aspiration and actual achievement undreamed of by the vanished peoples of bygone times.

At first sight, to be sure, much of their effort appears to be irreparably, even wantonly, destructive, and perhaps nowhere more so than in the blows they have dealt at the traditional conception of the central fact in man's psychical make-up—that intangible entity variously known as the ego, the self, the personality, animated and governed by an indwelling, unifying principle, the soul. Every man instinctively believes that there is only one of him. He feels that, no matter how his thoughts, his sensations, his emotions may change in the course of time, he himself will remain essentially and permanently the same. Putting this belief into metaphysical language, he declares, with the excellent Thomas Reid:

"The conviction which every man has of his identity ... needs no aid of philosophy to strengthen it; and no philosophy can weaken it without first producing some degree of insanity.... The identity of a person is a perfect identity; wherever it is real it admits of no degrees; and it is impossible that a person should be in part the same and in part different, because a person is a monad, and is not divisible into parts."[45]

But the modern explorer of the nature of man, replies:

"You are wrong, my friend. Your self is very far from being the simple, stable unity that you imagine it to be. In reality it is most complex and most unstable, easily breaking up, and sometimes breaking up so completely that it may even be replaced by an entirely new self. You do not believe this? I can prove it to you from

[45] Thomas Reid's "Essay on the Intellectual Powers of Man," pp. 228-231 (James Walker's edition of 1850).

the facts not only of scientific experiment, but also of everyday observation."

Naturally, in support of this statement, stress would be laid on instances resembling the strange case of BCA, just narrated. And although cases at all similar to the BCA affair are extremely uncommon there are a number on record evidencing in other ways so-called "total dissociation of personality." For example:

A prosperous Philadelphia plumber, a man of exemplary habits and seemingly in good health, left his home one day to take a short walk. From that moment he disappeared as completely as though the earth had opened and swallowed him. There was no reason why he should abscond or commit suicide, and the general belief was that he had met with foul play. Rewards were offered, and detectives employed, but no trace of him could be found. His wife, giving him up for dead, sold his business and removed with their children to Chicago.

Nearly two years later, the workmen in a tin-shop in a Southern city were startled one morning by the conduct of one of their number, who, dropping his tools and pressing his hand to his head in a bewildered way, sprang to his feet, and cried:

"My God! Where am I? How did I get here? This isn't my shop!"

The foreman, thinking he was drunk, or had gone insane, ran forward to pacify him.

"Steady, Smith, steady!" he exclaimed. "You'll be all right in a minute."

The other only stared at him wildly.

"Why do you call me Smith?" he demanded. "That isn't my name."

"That's the name you've gone by since you came among us six months ago."

"Six months ago! You're crazy, man. It isn't half an hour since I left my wife and little ones to get a breath of fresh air before dinner."

"Look here," said the foreman, pressing him gently into a seat, "where do you suppose you are, anyway?"

"Why, in Philadelphia, of course."

It was indeed the Philadelphia plumber, whose missing self had returned to him as suddenly and as mysteriously as it had vanished. A few days more and he was happily reunited with the family that had so long believed him to be among the dead.[46]

Where, it may well be asked, was this man's original self during these two years? What had become of his normal ego, the ego of which alone he had formerly been aware? Yet at no time throughout the period when he lacked knowledge of his identity, and was without memory for his earlier life and social relationships, did he display the slightest sign of mental aberration. He was as sane and real to himself and to those with whom he came into contact, and was as able to take care of himself and earn a sufficient living, as he had ever been in the years before he

[46] Boris Sidis's "Multiple Personality," pp. 365-368. This book, by one of the foremost American psychopathologists, should be read by all students of abnormal psychology.

experienced the remarkable psychical upheaval that had substituted an alien, a "secondary" self in the place of the self he had always been and known.

A blow, an illness, a fright, the stress of a prolonged emotion—any one of several causes may bring about this weird condition, of which I could give illustrative cases to a number that would fill many pages of this book.[47] Sometimes, though fortunately seldom, there may be—as in the case of BCA—a double or even a multiple dissociation, resulting in the development of two, three, four, or more secondary selves, which alternate with one another in a way productive of the most intense mental agony to the helpless victim.

But, after all, it is not necessary to insist on such extreme instances in order to demonstrate the essential instability and divisibility of that which we commonly have in mind when we speak of the "self." Dissociation of personality is in evidence every day in the pathetic symptomatology of the various insanities, and in the chronic, if often masked and unrecognized, memory lapses universal among sufferers from the manifold affections of hysteria, such as we dealt with in the chapter on "Dissociation and Disease." It is in evidence in the victims of alcoholic and drug excesses, who, in a very literal sense, may become "another person," and say and do things quite alien from their usual self, and concerning which their usual self afterward has no knowledge.

Even normal sleep, albeit a wise provision for the rest and strengthening of the organism, involves dissociation. Still more strikingly is dissociation evident in the phenomena of the state of artificial sleep induced by hypnotism.

It would carry us too far from the point now under consideration to enter here into any discussion of the nature and mechanism of hypnotism, that still widely misunderstood but marvelous agency, not simply for therapeutic purposes but for the study and exploration of man's inmost being. The thing of immediate importance is the fact that under the influence of hypnotism a person invariably develops a self more or less different from his ordinary waking, conscious self.

Hypnotized, he is to all outward seeming oblivious to everything transpiring around him. But let the hypnotist speak to him, question him, and he instantly responds with answers so intelligent as to indicate that, in some respects, at all events, he is more alert and keen than when wide awake. Curiously enough, however, commands and suggestions given to him are, within certain limitations, accepted and acted upon, no matter how disagreeable or absurd they may be.

Later, when awakened, he is in precisely the same position as are victims of spontaneous dissociation—such as the Philadelphia plumber, and Doctor Prince's puzzling neurasthene, BCA. That is to say, he is unable to give any account of what he has said and done during hypnosis. Thus the effect of hypnotism is to produce a psychical cleavage so profound as to involve the action, within a single organism, of two separate selves.

This has been demonstrated by a long line of scientific investigators, including physicians and psychologists of international reputation. Moreover, these investi-

[47] A collection of such cases will be found in my book, "Scientific Mental Healing," pp. 124-155.

gators have shown that, even after a person has been brought out of the hypnotic state, the self evoked by hypnotism may in some inscrutable way continue operant without his suspecting for a moment its existence and influence.

Impressive proof of this is found in the execution of what are known as post-hypnotic commands. A hypnotized person is told that, after being de-hypnotized, he is to perform a certain act on receiving a certain signal, or at the expiration of a certain time. As usual, when restored to his conscious, waking state, he remembers nothing of the command imposed on him; but when the signal is given, or the appointed time arrives, he feels an irresistible, and to him inexplicable, impulse to carry out the suggested idea.

Thus, in one series of fifty-five experiments made by the foremost English authority on hypnotism, Doctor J. Milne Bramwell, the subject, a young woman of nineteen, was ordered to perform a specified act at the end of a varying number of minutes, ranging from three hundred to more than twenty thousand. Not once, on being de-hypnotized, did she remember what she had been told to do, although offered a liberal reward if she could recall the commands given her.

Nevertheless, only two of the fifty-five experiments were complete failures, while in forty-five she executed the commands at exactly the moment designated, and in the remainder was at no time more than five minutes out of the way. As to the complete failures, Doctor Bramwell ascertained that in one instance she had mistaken the suggestion given, and in the other the circumstances were such that the command might have been executed without his being aware of it.[48]

Equally astonishing results are reported by the brilliant group of Frenchmen who, uniting under the direction of Doctor A. A. Liébeault, were the first to make an organized investigation of the cause and effects, the possibilities and limitations, of hypnotism. One of these French investigators, Doctor Hippolyte Bernheim, once hypnotized an old soldier, and asked him:

"On what day in the first week of October will you be at liberty?"

"On the Wednesday."

"Well," said Doctor Bernheim, "on that day you will pay a visit to Doctor Liébeault; you will find in his office the president of the republic, who will present you with a medal and a pension."

The soldier was then awakened and questioned as to what had been said to him, but could remember nothing. However, on Wednesday, October 3, Doctor Liébeault wrote to Doctor Bernheim:

"Your soldier has just called at my house. He walked to my bookcase, and made a respectful salute; then I heard him utter the words: 'Your excellency!' Soon he held out his right hand, and said: 'Thanks, your excellency.' I asked him to whom he was speaking. 'Why, to the president of the republic.' He turned again to the bookcase and saluted, then went away. The witnesses to the scene naturally asked me what that madman was doing. I answered that he was not mad, but as

[48] These experiments by Doctor Bramwell were first reported by him in the Proceedings of the Society for Psychical Research, vol. xii, pp. 176-203.

reasonable as they or I, only another person was acting in him."[49]

Compare with this an amusing little story told by Doctor Prince.

"Wishing to test the compelling influence of post-hypnotic commands," he says,[50] "I suggested to one of my subjects, Mrs. R., after she was hypnotized, that on the following day, when she went down to dinner, she would put on her bonnet, and keep it on during the whole of dinner time. The next day I received a letter from her in which she said:

"'I think I am getting insane. At dinner time I would wear my hat during the meal.'

"On further inquiry, I obtained the following story, which I give substantially in the original language:

"'As I was going in to dinner, my girl asked me what I was going out for. "I am not," says I. "I am going to eat my dinner." "Then what have you got your hat on for?" says she. I put my hand to my head, and there was my bonnet. "Lord, Mamie!" says I, "am I going crazy?" "No, mother," she says, "you often do foolish things." I began to get frightened, but took off my bonnet and went into the next room to dinner.'

"Then the younger child similarly asked her where she was going, and called attention to her having her bonnet on. A second time she raised her hand to her head, and to her surprise found that her bonnet was really there. She again took it off, and later, when her husband entered, the same thing was repeated; but when she found her bonnet on her head for the third time, she made excuse of the stormy words that ensued to declare she would 'keep it on now till she was through.' After dinner, being alarmed, she consulted a neighbor about it."

But the longest time on record for the carrying out of a post-hypnotic suggestion was made by a subject of Doctor Liégeois, another of the early French investigators. Doctor Liégeois hypnotized a young man, and said to him:

"A year from to-day this is what you are going to do, and what you are going to see: You will call at Doctor Liébeault's office in the morning, and tell him that you have come to thank him and Doctor Liégeois for all they have done to improve your health. While you are talking to him, you will see enter the room a dog with a monkey riding on its back. They will perform a thousand tricks that will amuse you very much.

"Then you will see a man come in, leading a great American grizzly bear, which will also perform tricks. It will be a tame bear, so that you will not be at all frightened. The man will be delighted at recovering his trained dog and monkey, which he thought he had lost. Before he leaves you will borrow a few cents from Doctor Liébeault to give to him."

Doctor Liégeois, after repeating these complicated and absurd directions, awoke the young man, and by cautious questioning ascertained that his memory

[49] "De la Suggestion dans l'État Hypnotique," p. 29.

[50] Boston Medical and Surgical Journal, vol. cxxii, p. 463.

was a perfect blank for all that had been said to him while he was hypnotized. Great care was taken not to recall to his mind at any time the command given to him, and which his hypnotic self was expected to remember and perform on the appointed day.

Exactly a year later, at nine in the morning, Doctor Liégeois went to Doctor Liébeault's office, where he waited half an hour, and then returned home, thinking that the experiment had failed. But at ten minutes to ten the young man arrived. There was nothing about his appearance to indicate that he was in any abnormal condition.

He greeted Doctor Liébeault, explained that he had come to thank him for his kindness to him, and inquired for Doctor Liégeois, whom he said he had expected to find there. A few minutes afterward, Doctor Liégeois having meanwhile been hastily summoned, the young man cried out that a monkey had just come in, riding on the back of a dog. He watched the antics of these imaginary animals with great interest, laughing heartily, and describing the tricks he fancied he saw them performing. After this, he announced the arrival of a man who was evidently the owner of the monkey and the dog, and he begged Doctor Liébeault to lend him a little money to reward the man for the amusement his animals had given him. But he saw no bear.

A moment later he was conversing with the two physicians, in evident ignorance of all that he had just been saying and doing. He angrily denied that there had been any animals in the room. When asked why he himself was there, he could give no definite reply. Doctor Liégeois immediately put him into the hypnotic state, and demanded:

"Do you know why you came here this morning?"

"Of course I do."

"Why was it?"

"Because you told me to."

"When?"

"A year ago."

"But you did not come at nine o'clock?"

"You did not tell me to come at nine o'clock. You said to come at exactly a year from the time you were talking to me. It was ten minutes to ten when you gave me your command."

"And why did you not see the bear?"

"Because you said nothing about a bear when you repeated your orders. You spoke only once of a bear. Everything else you spoke of twice. I thought you had changed your mind about the bear."[51]

---

[51] Dr. Liégeois's account of his many hypnotic experiments, as given in his "De la Suggestion et du Somnambulisme dans leurs Rapports avec la Jurisprudence et la Médecine légale," forms one of the most striking contributions to the literature of hypnotism.

Obviously, the hypnotic self, distinct and different though it is from the primary, waking self, can reason, can analyze, can draw conclusions as readily as the conscious self, and is, to put it otherwise, as truly a self as the conscious self.

Facts like these, as was said, have caused numerous investigators to question the validity of the hitherto prevailing view of human personality. The self, they affirm, is no single, continuous, permanent entity. On the contrary, it is merely a loosely coördinated aggregation of mental states, forever shifting and changing, so that the self of to-morrow may be vastly different from the self of to-day. To quote Professor Ribot, the famous scientist, and one of the most distinguished exponents of this new view of the self:

"The unity of the ego is not the unity of a single entity diffusing itself among multiple phenomena; it is the coördination of a certain number of states perpetually renascent, and having for their sole, common basis the vague feeling of the body. This unity does not diffuse itself downward, but is aggregated by ascent from below; it is not an initial, but a terminal point."

And Ribot adds emphatically:

"It is the organism, with the brain, its supreme representative, which constitutes the real personality; comprising in itself the remains of all that we have been and the possibilities of all that we shall be. The whole individual character is there inscribed, with its active and passive aptitudes, its sympathies and antipathies, its genius, its talent or its stupidity, its virtues and its vices, its torpor or its activity."[52]

Or, as the eminent psychologist, Alfred Binet, declares:

"We have long been accustomed by habits of speech, fictions of law, and also by the results of introspection, to consider each person as constituting an indivisible unity. Actual researches utterly modify this current notion. It seems to be well proven nowadays that if the unity of the ego be real, a quite different definition should be applied to it. It is not a single entity; for, if it were, one could not understand how in certain circumstances some patients, by exaggerating a phenomenon which obviously belongs to normal life, can unfold several different personalities. A thing that can be divided must consist of several parts. Should a personality be able to become double or triple, this would be proof that it is compound, a grouping of, and a resultant from, several elements."[53]

But the brain, which Ribot identifies with the personality, is a mere organ of the body, perishing with the body. Does it follow that the self perishes with bodily death? Is it really without an abiding, indwelling principle superior to, and independent of, the physical organism—in short, a soul—that would enable it to survive the final catastrophe of earthly existence? Is man soulless? Does death end personality?

Aye, those who hold with Ribot would reply. To speak of a soul is, in their

[52] Ribot's "Les Maladies de la Personalité." Quoted from F. W. H. Myers's translation in his "Human Personality and its Survival of Bodily Death," vol. i, p. 10.

[53] "Les Altérations de la Personnalité," p. 316.

view of the case, sheer mysticism, since "the ego in us is nothing more than the functional result of the arrangement for the time being of the molecules or ions of our brain matter."

That is why, at the beginning of this chapter, I stated that, of all the labors of the modern investigators of the nature of man, none would seem to be so irreparably destructive as the blows they have dealt at the traditional conception of human personality.

Yet, when we probe a little deeper, it will be found that the damage is not so irreparable as would at first appear; nay, it will even be found that by their searching inquiries, the advocates of the brain-stuff theory have unwittingly provided stronger reasons than were at any previous time available for insisting both on the actuality of the soul and the fundamental unity and continuity of the ego.

Undeniably, it is necessary to modify the old conception in some important respects. After the discoveries that have been made as to the disintegrating effects of natural and artificially induced sleep, of disease, of sudden frights, of profound emotional shocks, of alcohol and drugs, etc., it is idle to pretend that unity and continuity are distinctive characteristics of the ordinary self of waking life. So far as that self is concerned, its instability and divisibility are now plainly evident.

What, however, if it can be shown that, equally with the secondary selves that may and so often do replace it, the primary self is only part of a larger self—a self which persists unchanged beneath all the mutations of spontaneous and experimental occurrence? In that case it will at once become clear that the situation has again changed completely, and that we are back to the traditional, the intuitive, the "common-sense" conception of personality, with the single difference that the term "self" means something broader and nobler than when we limit it to the now demonstrated unstable, and ever-changeable self of ordinary consciousness.

And it is precisely to such a view of the self that the discoveries of the modern investigators, when closely scrutinized, irresistibly impel us. If, I repeat, they have shown that what we usually look upon as the self is liable to sudden extinction, they have likewise brought to light abundant evidence to prove that there is none the less an abiding self, a self not dominated by but dominating the organism, and unaffected by any vicissitudes that may befall the organism.

To be sure, it must be said that, as yet, comparatively few of those to whom we owe this evidence are prepared to admit that such is the ultimate outcome of their efforts. All the same, the evidence is there, not simply justifying, but rendering logically necessary, the hypothesis of a continuous, unitary ego, inclusive of, and superior to, all changing selves of outward manifestation, and possessing powers thus far little utilized; but, under certain conditions, utilizable for our material, intellectual, and moral betterment.

I have, in fact, in the previous chapters presented much of the evidence supporting this view.[54] All the phenomena of subconscious mental action—as variously exhibited in telepathy, crystal vision, automatic writing and speaking, the cure of disease by wholly mental means—point unmistakably, I am persuaded, to

[54] See also my book, "The Riddle of Personality," especially pp. 69-70, 159-162.

the existence of a superior self to which the ordinary self of everyday life stands in much the same relation as does the secondary self of a hysterical patient to the ordinary, normal self of a healthy person.

Not all the faculties of the larger self—for instance, the faculty involved in telepathic action—seem to be adapted for ready employment here on earth. Which would argue, of course, for a future state in which, freed from all hampering limitations of the body, such faculties will have full manifestation.

But most assuredly, as the findings of the psychopathologists indicate plainly, some among these hidden powers are amply available for use here and now, and may be so employed as to enable the self of ordinary consciousness to become less liable to disintegration, to ward off and conquer disease, to develop mental attainments of a high order, to solve life's varying problems with a sureness and success sadly lacking to most of us at present.

INDEX

Lector House believes that a society develops through a two-fold approach of continuous learning and adaptation, which is derived from the study of classic literary works spread across the historic timeline of literature records. Therefore, we aim at reviving, repairing and redeveloping all those inaccessible or damaged but historically as well as culturally important literature across subjects so that the future generations may have an opportunity to study and learn from past works to embark upon a journey of creating a better future.

This book is a result of an effort made by Lector House towards making a contribution to the preservation and repair of original ancient works which might hold historical significance to the approach of continuous learning across subjects.

HAPPY READING & LEARNING!

LECTOR HOUSE LLP
E-MAIL: lectorpublishing@gmail.com

9 789353 422400

Lightning Source UK Ltd.
Milton Keynes UK
UKHW041154280919
350541UK00012B/106/P

9 789353 422400